Devotionals from Accounting Classes

by

Dr. Roger L. Stichter

ISBN: 978-1-790-38656-7

I dedicate this book to the hundreds of students who have taken classes from me over the more than twenty years I have taught Accounting at Grace College.

Introduction and Acknowledgements

I first came to Grace College as a full-time Accounting professor in January 1995. The first semester that I taught college courses, I prayed before each class – which was what was expected by this Christ-centered college. But these prayers soon seemed repetitive and didn't add much value to the college experience for neither my students nor me. After considering this for a time, I decided to incorporate my life into both my teaching and how I began class each day. I started sharing some of my experiences, both historical and more recent, and tying these experiences into biblical principles hoping my students would retain both the Accounting knowledge better and have something to encourage them spiritually.

It worked! Students began positively mentioning these devotionals in course evaluations. I like positive feedback so I worked harder at developing devotionals that helped students. Then, students began asking if they could have my devotionals. I didn't have any of them written down as I just presented each devotional from a scripture reference and a few notes I kept.

The following book comprises most of the devotionals I give in each class I teach. I incorporated three devotionals I don't use as often to make an even 50 devotionals in this book. One series of devotionals is missing. The devotionals I give in Intermediate Accounting II uses another book which I was denied permission to use without cost and I have decided to not include these devotionals in the first edition of this book. The book is separated into the classes I teach and most devotionals are presented in the order I give them during the semester. One devotional is used per week of class.

I want to thank my wife, Jane, for her suggestions, comments, and encouragement. I spent an entire Christmas break writing both these devotionals and on another book I have written with not much time at home that "break". She has been my constant support and keeps me more humble than I would be without her. Zach and Amy Evans also provided suggestions and found (hopefully) most of my grammatical errors. I appreciate the time they took while being a busy father, mother, husband, and wife. I thank my students for their support and encouragement. I would not be giving devotionals without them and would not have written this book without their continued encouragement. Most of all, I thank God for leading me to the career of Accounting Professor. It seems to fit my God-given gifts well and I'm so glad I listened to the call, both times, to teach college.

I am deeply grateful to my wife of 35+ years, Jane, and my children and their spouses: Adam and Anne, Luke, Jeremiah and Stacey, Susanna and Peter, Rebecca (deceased), Jubilee, Angella, and Jericho. They played a role in many of the stories in these devotionals and have shaped my life greatly. I hope you enjoy recalling some devotionals you heard in class or reading them for the first time.

Roger

Contents

Devotionals given in Financial Accounting.. 2

Devotionals given in Managerial Accounting...................................... 28

Devotionals given in Intermediate Accounting I............................... 48

Devotionals given in Advanced Accounting..................................... 76

Some final devotionals.. 96

Devotionals given in Financial Accounting

The following devotionals are generally used in the first accounting class students take while in college. The overall emphasis of the devotionals is the concept of obedience. For the Christian, God is owed our obedience. I firmly believe that obedience is the highest form of worship.

The Feed Wagon

I Samuel 15:22

James 2:10

Part of growing up on a farm was raising cattle. "Feeder cattle" were ones you raised from a fairly young age until they were ready to butcher. Most feeder cattle were kept in a pretty small fenced in space and fed grain so they would gain weight quickly without running the weight off in an open field. For little kids, the feed wagon made a great sandbox. The feed in the wagon had been ground up into a rather fine mixture of grains making it a very soft place to play.

One day my dad made a pretty direct point to my brother and me to stop playing in the feed wagon because we were bringing feed into the house in our pants and making a mess. I'm sure my mom had something to do with my dad's directive. Since jeans back then weren't sized the way they are today, we rolled our pant legs up to the needed length instead of just buying jeans that were the right length for us. We must have carried enough feed into the house in our pockets and pant cuffs that my mom got tired of cleaning up after us and my dad told us to stop.

I'm sure we heard all of what Dad said but we must have interpreted it to mean we just weren't to bring any more feed into the house.

One day, one of my uncles stopped by our house and observed my brother and me playing in the feed wagon. He went directly to my dad and told him there were two little boys playing in the feed wagon and they were totally naked! My dad, with his quick wit, told my uncle they must be the neighbor boys. As I recall, we didn't have any neighbor boys who came to our house. I don't remember how this story totally ended but I'm sure we never played in the feed wagon again!

Most of us aren't much different than my brother and I were in this story. When we don't like the exact directives we are given, we think of ways to try and get around them. King Saul did this as described in I Samuel 15. He did part of what God directed but not exactly all that God directed and then Saul seems to boast about his own "obedience". The prophet Samuel was given the task of confronting Saul. As part of this confrontation, Samuel reveals part of the heart of God saying that God is seeking total obedience. Saul tried to justify what he had done by stating he had not totally obeyed so that he had something to offer as a sacrifice to God in worship. Samuel states that obedience means more to God than our acts of worship.

As I have contemplated this over the years, I have come to the understanding that obedience is actually worship! I tell my students that obedience is the highest form of worship. When our hearts are desiring to obey God in every aspect of our lives, we are worshipping. As a parent, I understand this concept. When my children obeyed our house rules without needing to be reminded, my wife and I were honored. But when our children would disobey or only do part of what we wanted, we were dishonored. I believe God feels the same way. Obedience is the highest form of worship.

God Credits Our Account

Philippians 4:10-17

Accountants like things to balance. Debits and Credits are used to achieve balance in accounting. Accounting also utilizes an equation to maintain this balance. The equation is: Assets = Liabilities + Owner's Equity. The equation may be translated as what we own equals what we owe plus what we are worth. The asset side of this equation is increased by debiting accounts and the liability side of the equation is increased by crediting accounts.

Most of us have some understanding of this equation because when we put money in our bank accounts, the bank credits our account. To the bank, our account is a liability. The bank owes the money back to us. When the bank pays us interest we have earned on our deposited money, the bank credits our account. The opposite is also true. If we incur fees, the bank debits our account to take the fees out of our account.

The Apostle Paul must have understood this concept. In Philippians 4, Paul commends the Philippians for their concern for him and for how generously they shared financial gifts with Paul. Then Paul makes an interesting statement. In verse 17, Paul states that he desires "more be credited to your account". Paul says he has been "amply supplied" and has enough for his own needs. Then Paul looks ahead to the future reward God will give the Philippians, and he desires that they receive an even greater reward.

Paul seems to be saying that when we are generous in meeting the needs of others, God increases something owed to us. Just as the money we deposit into a bank account is owed back to us, when we make deposits by being generous, God owes something back to us. I've often wondered how God intends to pay us back what is owed to us. Are these the crowns talked about in Revelation? Is there another method God will use to repay us out of the account?

But what if we aren't generous and don't build up a balance in our account? I believe we will be tremendously embarrassed if we don't have much in our account when God reveals to us (and to everyone else) how we have used the time and talents He provided for us. If we spend most of God's money to buy stuff for our own use and pleasure and are not generously sharing with those in need, God has no way to credit our account. Studies continue to confirm that Christians in the United States only donate about 3% of their income to both the church and other charities. Whether you believe the tithe is biblical or not, 3% is a very tiny percentage when we understand the extreme wealth of our culture.

There are approximately 325 million people living in the United States. If only 15% are devoted Christians and a family is assumed to be 5 people, there are about 50 million people living in devoted Christian families and about 10 million families (325 million x 15% divided by 5). If the average family income is $50,000 a year for these families and each family gave only 1% more of their income per year, this would equate to $5 billion more giving per year. Every extra 1% in giving equals close to $5 billion extra per year to maintain churches, help the poor, and reach the world with the gospel. If the church in just the United States gave 10% instead of 3%, that would be an extra $35 billion per year. How long would it take to reach the whole world with the gospel if Christians would give just 10%? Probably not very long and Christians would be putting much larger credits into their heavenly account.

Jesus Validated the Tithe

Matthew 23: 23-28

It must have been my 10th birthday because I had just received $10 as a gift. That was the most money I had ever had in my life. Back in the late 1960's, candy bars cost five cents each and my $10 amounted to about 200 candy bars. I was rich!

During that time in my life, we lived just outside of town in a plantation-style house that was white, square, two-story, and had four large, square pillars in the front of the house that reached from the porch to the top of the second story of the house. The back room of the house stretch the entire length of the house with large windows that went from floor to ceiling and across the entire back wall. About half of the interior wall of that room was a limestone fireplace with a limestone hearth. I remember sitting with my mom on that hearth. She said something like this, "Now you know, Roger, the Bible teaches us that we should tithe from what we receive. That means a dollar of this $10 should be given back to God's work."

I was devastated! One whole dollar was 20 candy bars which would have supplied me for at least a few days. For some reason, that feeling of devastation is still clear in my mind today. I don't recall anything else my mom said or did but I know she left the decision up to me. I don't remember where I tithed, but I know I gave that dollar. To this day, I believe that was the pivotal decision point in my life as to whether or not I would tithe. Since then, I have never struggled to give the tithe. Even when I was borrowing money to go to college, I tithed from money I earned working various jobs and I have always had enough money to live on.

While I know there are some who say the tithe was an Old Testament concept and is no longer valid, I believe Jesus validated the tithe in Matthew 23:23 as a continuing concept when he told the Pharisees that they should not be neglecting the tithe. There definitely were some things the Pharisees were missing but Jesus seems to say they should continue to tithe. Jesus goes on to say the Pharisees are full of greed and self-indulgence. I wonder if justifying not tithing is a statement that our inside is similarly full of greed and self-indulgence. Certainly our society pushes us this way. How much of what we buy is really needed? How much is because we just want things that we believe will make us happy? Tithing seems to be a recognition of God's ownership over all we have. While I believe almost all of us have the ability, and maybe the need, to give much more than 10%, there is no doubt in my mind that giving the tithe is one way we are totally obedient to God and truly worship.

So much of what Jesus said was countercultural. When teaching about God's heart, Jesus went far beyond the law and said our motivation is important. We don't need to kill someone to commit murder in God's eyes, hating others is equivalent. We don't need to commit adultery to sin, contemplating the act is equivalent. If the tithe was what was accepted as donating enough to the Jews, it seems that Jesus would have gone beyond that. I believe God owns it all and, instead of deciding how much to give, we need to decide how much we keep to live on. It is probably far less than most of us believe we need which frees up much more to give and add to our heavenly credit.

Children and the Rich

Mark 10:13-27

I have learned that the authors of the Gospels did not always put everything in chronological order, instead they put things in a certain order to better tell the story and to convey the message they wanted to get across. In three of the gospels, Matthew, Mark, and Luke, there are two stories that are always written together. The first is where the disciples try to keep little children from bothering Jesus and the second is the story of the rich, young ruler who asks Jesus what he must do to inherit eternal life. Jesus rebukes the disciples for trying to keep children away from him and states that "the kingdom belongs to such as these." Jesus also stated that we must receive the kingdom like children in order to enter the kingdom.

When the young, rich man asked Jesus what he must do, Jesus lists off five of the ten commandments and states that he should not defraud. The man responds that he has kept those six things since he was young. Of the five commandments that Jesus does not list, four are ones I believe would have been kept by nearly every Jewish person: no other gods before me; no graven image; not take the name of God in vain; remember the Sabbath. These commandments should go without mentioning. But one commandment was left out and seemed to be the issue of this man's heart – greed. The tenth commandment listed in Exodus 20 deals with coveting or wanting things that aren't yours. This man apparently viewed his wealth as his and did not have the attitude that he was simply a steward of it for God. When told that the only way to inherit eternal life was to release his grip on wealth, he couldn't do it.

In these two stories we see a vivid contrast between the tendencies of children and the tendencies of the rich. While we could probably each come up with a list of things we believe are valued by children and things we believe are valued by the rich, I believe it boils down

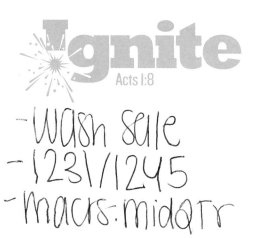

Ignite
Acts 1:8

- wash sale
- 1231/1245
- macrs: midQtr

to two big issues: stuff vs relationship and dependence vs independence.

Most children don't actually own much stuff. When kids who grew up in a wealthy household whose parents were gone a lot to meet the demands of their jobs are asked what they most wanted while growing up, most reply that they wished they had more time with their parents, or, relationship. Children value relationship. If we boil down what rich people value it often comes down to stuff. This is why, in the United States, the rich give a lower percentage of their income away than poorer people give away - there is always more stuff to buy and greed takes over.

The other issue is one of dependence. Children are totally dependent on someone to take care of them. Without care, children die. The rich are opposite. They are independent. The "American Dream" boils down to generating enough wealth that we don't need to depend on anyone. This seems totally opposite to what God intended. God wants us to be dependent on Him. This doesn't mean we don't make money, it means we don't accumulate so much that we try to protect ourselves from anything that could go wrong. We need to see ourselves as dependent on God, because we are.

Jesus was all about relationship and being dependent on God. If Jesus is a representation of God in human flesh, and I believe he is, Jesus is stating that God values relationship more than stuff. If we value stuff more than relationship, we aren't in the Kingdom. While there is never any other mention in scripture of giving everything away, Jesus does mention that we need to get rid of things (or even body parts) that are causing us to sin. Valuing stuff more than relationship is sin. Desiring to be independent rather than dependent is sin. Are you like a child?

Hard for the Rich

Mark 10:23-31

Right after the young, rich man walked away from Jesus because he couldn't give everything away as Jesus asked him to do, Jesus makes a statement that shocked the disciples. He said, "How hard it is for the rich to enter the kingdom of God!" This shocked the disciples because, in their culture, being rich was a sign that God's favor was on you. You were a shoe-in for the kingdom if you were rich. The poor weren't as lucky. But Jesus, as he was prone to do, reversed things. He said that it is really hard for the rich to enter the kingdom.

As the disciples were trying to digest that heretical statement, Jesus says more. He says it is easier to stuff a camel through the eye of a needle than for the rich to enter the kingdom. Now, most of us realize this is impossible. You just can't fit a camel through the eye of a needle, even if it is a very small camel and a very large needle.

I don't believe Jesus was talking about the Eye of the Needle gate in Jerusalem, as some have suggested, because the disciples were "even more amazed" when Jesus talked about the camel and needle. It was possible for a camel to get through the Eye of the Needle gate; it just took a lot more work. The disciples said something next that showed what Jesus had just stated was impossible. Jesus goes on to say that it is only possible for the rich to enter the kingdom by God's working because "all things are possible with God."

If we are honest with ourselves, nearly all of us living in the United States are rich. We don't feel rich because advertising keeps showing us how much we could still have. But if we compare ourselves to our world's population, we are extremely rich. When I compare my income to the average income of people around the world, I'm in the top 1%. As I'm writing this, an annual income of $33,000 per year is the top 1% and I'm way over that. Most of us are. If I take Jesus seriously, his words should scare me. It is hard for me to enter the kingdom. From what I can tell from the story of the young, rich man, if I don't release my grip on the riches I have, I can't enter the kingdom.

Peter, spokesman for the disciples and probably looking for some affirmation, reminds Jesus that they have left everything to follow Him. Jesus states that those who leave things, and even people, behind to follow Him will receive great riches now and eternal life. Some have interpreted this to mean we should be materially rich now. But then we would, again, be rich. I believe Jesus is saying we need to have an open hand with what we have and realize we don't really own it. This is a continual choice. We need to be totally willing to give it all away over and over again. Only then do we become totally dependent on God. Being dependent, just as little children are dependent, is the posture we need to enter the kingdom. Are you willing to release your grip on stuff?

Life Isn't Fair

Matthew 20:1-16

In Matthew's gospel, we find a parable where a landowner hires workers all throughout the day and pays them the same wage even though they didn't all work the same length of time. Since he starts by first paying those who worked a shorter length of time, the workers who worked all day expect to be paid more. But, when they receive an amount equal to those who worked a much shorter length of time, they complain to the landowner. The landowner answered by stating he paid the workers who worked all day the amount that was agreed upon when they started work that day. Therefore, they were not being treated unfairly. The landowner asks whether he has the right to do with his money what he wants. He also asks the workers whether they are envious because he was generous.

If I'm honest with myself, I relate better to the dissatisfaction of the workers who worked all day and received an amount equal to those who worked much less. I like to think that fairness is a right and, when I don't believe I have been treated fairly, I complain too. But life isn't fair. I find nothing in the Bible which states that God is fair. God is many things but fair is never mentioned in the Bible as one of His attributes. Our fifth child, Rebecca, was born with many "issues" which caused her to spend about 21 of the 26 months of her life at Riley Children's Hospital in Indianapolis. Is that fair? Don't get me wrong, I wouldn't trade that experience for nearly anything. It has shaped me in good ways that I don't believe would have happened otherwise. But it wasn't fair that I had such a child and most other people don't.

When I think about fairness long enough, I begin to realize that I'm usually on the good side of fair. I don't worry about my next meal or where I will sleep at night. I don't worry about whether I can afford going to the doctor or where I can find clean water to drink. My children have access to good education and all of my older children this isn't the case for many people in the world. ⟨...⟩n't even have clean water to drink and might only ⟨...⟩ay, let alone having access to health care.

⟨...⟩ this, I wonder if I am really generous. Or, do I just ⟨...⟩ave for myself with little concern for so many other ⟨...⟩don't have very much. The parable in Matthew 20 is about ⟨...⟩ It begins in verse 1: "For the kingdom of heaven is like a landowner…" God is generous. If I want to be more like Jesus (who was the representation of God in human flesh), I, also, need to be generous. I need to stop complaining that life isn't fair and start being more generous.

Transforming of my Mind

Philippians 4:4-9

I love rock music. It was part of my generation of the 70's. I knew my parents weren't too happy with how their boys listened to that music but it became part of who I was. Honestly, I love about all types of music but the rhythm of rock really got my attention.

When I was in my early 20's, I was confronted with the passage in Philippians 4, and especially verse 8, where Paul encourages the Philippians to think about things that are true, noble, right, pure, lovely, admirable, excellent, or praiseworthy. I knew that wasn't what was usually going through my mind. Thoughts of sex, swearing, drugs, and other behaviors that I, honestly, didn't partake in, were often at the front of my mind. I would wake up in the morning and these ungodly thoughts would pop into my mind.

So, I did something radical, for me anyway. I decided to give up rock music. I stopped listening to any secular music and had my radio tuned to the only Christian station we had in Northern Indiana (that I knew of) at the time. I could have never anticipated what happened next. I began waking up in the mornings with thoughts more focused on God, the person of Jesus, and worship. My mind was being transformed. Honestly, I was shocked by how quickly and radically the transformation happened. I no longer had to fight off thoughts of things I knew God didn't approve of and that I really didn't want to do anyway. It truly was a radical transformation of my mind.

I believe we have it harder today. Not only is there music which puts thoughts contrary to Philippians 4 into our minds, but there is also so much visual junk we can access. Video games, the internet, television shows, etc are so much more prevalent and graphic than what was available when I was young. I believe the combination of audio and visual junk we have access to has had a huge impact on our thinking and takes our minds away from what is excellent and praiseworthy.

We did not allow our children to play Teen-rated games because the visuals were just too graphic for what our family desired. We also did not visit Halloween theme shows or watch movies depicting magic or demonic activity. Once an image is in our minds, it is nearly impossible to not have it pop back up sometimes. The Bible talks a lot about not being controlled by fear. I know from seeing some scary scenes in movies when I was young that fearful scenes never leave your mind but they remain implanted even if you don't think about them often. I don't believe this is the type of thinking Paul was speaking about in Philippians 4.

Maybe you don't like what is going through your mind in the morning or throughout the day. I challenge you to do something radical and see how it transforms your mind.

My Dog Debit

John 4:27-38

I like to bicycle. I also like dogs and often had a dog as a child. Several years ago, I had decided our family was ready for a dog. As I bicycled on country roads one day, I saw a sign: "Beagle pups for sale". It didn't take many days for me to buy a cute beagle pup. While my children had several ideas for a name, I pondered what an accountant would call his dog and decided on the name Debit. In accrual accounting, debits increase asset accounts and also increase expense accounts. It seemed like a fitting name.

Later that summer, on the Saturday of Grace College's Welcome Weekend when freshmen first come to college, I took a long bike ride. I was several miles from home, behind schedule, and biking fast. As I came down a small hill into a little town, the minivan traveling toward me began to turn left, directly in my path. I was looking at the woman driving the minivan and she was looking at her front seat passenger, not at me. In the split second during which I surveyed the situation, I knew if I continued straight I would be hit by the minivan. There were two ATVs ahead of me sitting beside the road to my right. My only hope was to swerve right and brake as hard as possible to stop before hitting the ATVs and avoid hitting the minivan.

As I braked and swerved, I remember thinking "I've missed the van" but I don't recall the impact as my face hit the asphalt. I had several indicators that I hit the pavement pretty hard: my sunglasses had pebble scratches on them, the nosepiece of those glasses cut clear through my lip, and I had road rash (scraped up skin) on my face and shoulders. I remember people talking but I couldn't see anything until I was in the ambulance. After several hours in the ER, I began the slow process of recovery from the road rash, a broken hand, messed-up knee requiring surgery, and an extremely sore body. During this time, my children took care of Debit.

It was probably two weeks before I made my way to the barn to visit Debit. He had grown much larger and was happy to see me. I noticed a foul odor but couldn't figure out the source of the smell. The next day, as I spent more time with Debit, I again noticed the odor. It smelled like dead, rotting flesh. A closer examination of Debit revealed he had grown so much larger while I was recuperating that his collar had become too tight, had rubbed all the hair off of his neck under the collar, and was eating into the flesh on his neck. I felt sick inside as I carefully cut the collar off of Debit. The wound looked terrible and smelled even worse with the collar off. I genuinely thought he was going to die.

That night, after treating Debit's neck with some spray antibiotic I found at a pet store, I lay in bed, wide awake and hurting for my little puppy. I felt so badly for this dog that I couldn't fall asleep not knowing if he would be alive the next day. As I struggled with these feelings of pain, God broke into my thinking and clearly said, "You care so much about a dog that you can't even sleep but there are people all around you who smell of death and are going to Hell. You care more about a dog than you care about them." Wow! I cared more about a dog than I cared about my neighbors. Debit survived his ordeal but I will never forget God's clear reprimand.

Lost at Kmart

Luke 4:2-18

When I was a child, there weren't any malls or large shopping centers close to the farm where we lived. Most of our shopping was done in our local town. But sometimes we would drive to South Bend to do some shopping. My dad preferred to shop at Kmart where US 31 and US 20 now intersect. The Kmart is gone but the area still holds vivid memories for me.

When I was probably about 5 years old, my dad and an aunt and uncle of mine traveled to Kmart. I'm guessing it was close to Christmas time as the store was very busy. I remember being in the store with my dad walking around when, suddenly, he was gone. Somehow, we had gotten separated.

There was an intense feeling of anxiety as I experienced the need to find my father. I began walking around the store checking all the usual places we frequented at Kmart. I went to the sub shop as my dad almost always bought sub sandwiches when we went to Kmart; but he wasn't there. I went to the candy section because we always bought candy at Kmart; but he wasn't there. I don't remember every location I looked but I finally decided I would just go to the car and wait for my dad to find me there. This was before the days when locking your car was expected so I didn't have any trouble getting into the back seat of my uncle's car. I waited there for a long time – at least in my mind – until I realized they might not come out to the car to look. I remember leaving the car, opening and walking through the double glass doors at the main entrance to Kmart, and heading down the main isle. I didn't get very far until I realized my dad was there. I had found him. I don't recall what he said – whether he scolded me or said he was relieved to find me. I just recall my own relief at finally being found. I don't recall any more of this incident.

There are times in our Christian journey when we "lose" our Father. Sometimes it feels like God just isn't there as He was before. We tend to search for Him in the places where we usually sensed His presence before. These "places" could be a favorite devotional location, a special song, or a passage of scripture. But God may not be found there. As a dear lady in the church I grew up in explained so well one time, God sometimes hides His presence from us for a time. These times can be troubling for us as we frantically search for Him but He takes us through periods of testing to help us discover for ourselves how desperately we desire Him. In these times, His presence may not be sensed, but His is still with us! God wants to know we desire Him with all our heart. As we display this desire, He will not withhold His presence forever. He will reveal Himself to us at the appropriate time just as I found my father in Kmart so many years ago.

If God just isn't there like He used to be, don't despair. Keep pursuing Him. Let God know you will not give up on pursuing Him. When He is ready, He will be found. It probably won't be in the same way as you experienced God before but He will reveal Himself again.

Like a Child

Matthew 18:1-5

In Matthew 18, Jesus, when asked who was greatest in the kingdom of heaven states the one who takes a humble place, like a child, is greatest in the kingdom of heaven. Several years ago, one of my children modeled humility to me in a way I will never forget.

In our family, discipline happened for a number of transgressions but we spanked for only one thing – willful disobedience. I don't recall the exact issue of willful disobedience but it happened and I commanded the child to go to the bathroom for her spanking. This particular child is able to cry spontaneously so her crying was taking place before we made it to the bathroom. Our spankings are three whacks from a wide, smooth, plastic cutting board which stings but doesn't damage.

I administered the whacks, knelt down to look the child in the eye and opened my arms because children often desire affirmation immediately after their sentence has been carried out. Instead of falling into my arms, I was met with "Go away! I don't want to see you!" Ouch. That stung but I left the room and she did, too.

About 10 minutes later I was doing something in the kitchen when this child walked into the kitchen, came up to me, threw her arms around my legs and said, "I love you Daddy. I don't ever want you to leave." I knelt down and gave her a huge hug telling her I loved her, too, and I would never leave.

This interchange helps me understand what it means to take a humble place like a child. When our heavenly father disciplines us, we sometimes respond in hurt and anger. Our normal reaction may be to distance ourselves from the one we believe has hurt us. It is a humble heart which returns to our father, recognizes our need for discipline, and expresses our continued love. A child has a soft heart to discipline and does not stay angry for a long time.

I often wonder if my heart is that humble. Do I respond to God's discipline this way? Do I take a humble place in my interactions with others? Do I welcome the humble as Matthew 18:5 invites?

Healing my Knee

James 5:13-18

One of the injuries I sustained when I crashed my bicycle Welcome Weekend was a messed up knee. I use "clipless petals" and, apparently, my shoe didn't unclip soon enough and twisted my knee pretty good (or bad). When the orthopedic surgeon discussed my injuries with me, he took my leg and showed me how the part below the knee would move sideways independently of the top part of my leg. While it looked pretty cool, a knee isn't supposed to do that. Try it sometime.

The MRI of my knee also showed I had torn both sides of the meniscus in my knee. So, they scheduled surgery to clean up my knee. This would be the first surgery I had ever had performed on any of my body parts, so I asked my students to pray for me.

The day for surgery arrived and I got delayed. There was a bad accident in our town and the surgeon was called away for emergency surgeries. I finally got into surgery about 6 hours after my scheduled time. I remember counting backwards from 10. I think I got to 8 and I was out. Next thing I knew, someone was calling my name and I came out of the fog. It was about 15 minutes from the time I started counting backward. When the surgeon got into my knee, he found a perfect meniscus. No damage, nothing to do but take some junk out of my knee that had probably been there since I abused my body lifting heavy weights during high school athletics.

So, what happened? I asked the surgeon that question at my follow-up appointment and he reiterated that the MRI showed a torn meniscus – both sides. I was both upset (that I had surgery for no reason) and stoked! Had God chosen to heal my meniscus? What other explanation was there? The surgeon didn't offer that the MRI could have been wrong. He was pretty certain about that. I have chosen to believe that God healed my knee.

This wasn't the first time I had seen something unexplainable happen. Many years ago, my wife had chronic back problems. She got treatment of different kinds but the pain persisted. One evening we attended a joint worship evening where several churches met together for an evening of praise. In the middle of the worship time, one pastor stood up and said he believe God wanted to heal someone's back and asked people with back problems to come forward for prayer. My wife was one of a few who went forward. When she came back to her seat, she said her back felt better. Actually, it didn't just feel better, she didn't have any issues with it after that evening. God healed her back.

One day a student came to my office asking that I pray for his girlfriend who was staying at his parent's home due to a severe migraine headache that had persisted for days. I prayed for her and he left. A couple of hours later he showed up again, with her! She was healed. I don't take credit for that - God did it.

So, if God still heals today, why don't we ask for healing more often? We have a wonderful medical profession that God works through. But, in our society, even Christians don't usually ask God to heal first and use the medical profession secondarily. We use the medical profession first and ask God secondarily. Something about that seems backward.

Working on Sunday

Exodus 31:14-15

Matthew 12: 1-14

We live in the woods behind a row of houses. While driving home one day, I saw a pallet of shingles sitting at a neighbor's house and told my wife that someone was going to be putting new shingles on their house. Sure enough, one Saturday a couple of weeks later I heard hammering and saw people on the neighbor's roof.

Near evening, I walked over to that neighbor's house and asked how they were doing. After a pretty brief conversation with my neighbor, I realized there was no way he was going to get his roof finished that weekend. His "friends" were offering some help but it appeared none of them would be available on Sunday to help. I walked home with a heavy heart knowing I wanted to help but knowing it would be Sunday and I was raised in a family who didn't work on Sunday.

In the couple of minutes it took me to get home, I knew I needed to help him anyway. I told my wife and teenage sons that we were going to help our neighbor do his roof the next day. We were part of a church which met in "house" churches and church was to be at our house the next day. So, I called people in our house church and told them I was going to help my neighbor instead of being at the meeting. I invited them to help, but told them there was no pressure - I would totally understand if they decided not to help.

The next morning, I got my nail apron and hammer and walked to my neighbor's house. He was standing on the roof looking over things. I climbed the ladder and asked him who he had coming to help that day. He said that he didn't think anyone was coming to help. I told him I thought that I had a few people coming. His exact words were, "There is a God!" Then he said, "I didn't think you worked on Sunday." Honestly, I didn't think I worked on Sunday, either, but heard myself say something like "I believe Jesus taught that it was ok to do good on the Sabbath." My neighbor said, "I like that." Up on that roof on Sunday morning, we had church. The conversation for the next few minutes was about God and his care for us and how we help those we care about. It was pretty good stuff.

People started showing up. One man in our house church was a contractor and he brought his trailer with tools complete with air compressor and roofing nail guns. We had the roof done by mid-afternoon and it was a pretty good job. To this day, I can have a theological conversation anytime I want with that neighbor. I don't know where he is totally at with God, but I know he is closer to God now than he was before we helped on his roof. And, I grew in the process. It really is right to do good on the Sabbath, even if that means helping people put on their roof.

Choosing a spouse

I Samuel 15

I Samuel 15 is a chapter about King Saul's disobedience and arrogance. God asks Saul to destroy the Amalekites. The Amalekites had attacked Israel when Israel had left Egypt and was heading toward the Promised Land. God was finally distributing justice to the Amalekites. Saul was supposed to destroy everything associated with the Amalekites including all people and all livestock. Nothing was to be left alive. This directive is difficult to comprehend but God had reasons and asked Saul to carry them out.

Saul did most of what he was asked but not everything he was asked. He obeyed partially. Saul kept the Amalekite king, Agag, alive and kept some of the best of the livestock alive. God spoke to His prophet, Samuel, and told Samuel to find Saul. Saul had gone to Carmel, set up a monument in his own honor, and then traveled on to Gilgal where Samuel finally found Saul.

Saul was feeling pretty good about his victory (and himself) and thought God was going to feel just as good about his actions. But Samuel tells Saul that God is not pleased. When confronted as to why there were still livestock alive, Saul both blames the soldiers and says the livestock was kept to sacrifice to God. But Saul had already gone to Carmel and had not sacrificed to God. He had set up a monument to himself! Saul's excuse doesn't seem very likely to be totally true.

God wanted everything destroyed. In verses 22 and 23, Samuel tells Saul that God is more interested in total obedience than in sacrifice. When we don't totally obey, we sin against God - just as if we used witchcraft or worshipped idols. Those are very serious sins! The accusations against Saul were very serious, too. Samuel then tells Saul that God was taking the kingship away from Saul. His lack of obedience had caused God to reject him as king.

What does all this have to do with choosing a spouse? Well, I believe the best spouse is one who desires to be totally obedient to God. Young people are often drawn to spousal candidates who are pretty or handsome, are rich or have the ability to make a lot of money, and/or who use a lot of kind and flattering words. The physical characteristics draw us to others we might like to marry but, those of us who have been married for a while, know that our bodies change. Those physical characteristics will not keep us in relationships forever. In the same way, money does not keep us happy or cover up problems in marriage. A lot of very wealthy marriages end in divorce.

But a godly man or woman is someone with value for a lifetime. Who else do we want to be the father or mother of our children than someone who desires to be totally obedient to God? Who else do we want to walk with us through the difficulties in life than someone who desires to be totally obedient to God? We all makes mistakes and fail to be totally obedient at times. But, if you want to find the right spouse, find someone who desires to be totally obedient to God. And, if you want to be the best spouse, be totally obedient to God!

Devotionals given in Managerial Accounting

The focus on these devotionals is how to respond when suffering happens. All Christians deal with suffering. None of us are exempt. God uses suffering to refine us – if we let this process happen. If we fight against the lessons we can learn during suffering, we actually suffer more as our attitude toward God and life deteriorates.

Bad things happen to good people

Job 1

In March 1997, our fifth child, Rebecca, was born. Rebecca spent about 21 months of her 26-month life at Riley Children's Hospital in Indianapolis. She never developed past an "infant" stage of development. We learned many valuable lessons during this time of life. It was an extremely difficult time, but also an extremely good time. I believe I came to value the church so much more. Without God's people praying for us, encouraging us, and helping us, I don't know how we would have managed that span of life.

Rebecca was born with a three-chambered heart, her esophagus was not connected to her stomach, she had enlarged ureters allowing urine to back up and cause infections, and there were other issues necessitating many surgeries during her life. As far as we know, my wife and I had done nothing "wrong". Neither of us smoke or drink alcohol; we didn't do drugs. There was no medical reason Rebecca was born with so many issues. I guess you could say we were chosen.

Job's story is sort of like this. As we read through Job chapter 1, we find out that God thought highly of Job. God brings up Job to Satan and allows Satan to cause Job to suffer. Job loses nearly all his wealth and all his children, and is left with no real way to support himself. Why would such suffering happen to such a good man? Job appears to be an excellent, godly father. His sons would invite their sisters to parties. I think this says something about the way Job raised his children during a time when men dominated most of society. His sons respected and honored their sisters. I doubt the boys learned this from their society. They had to learn it from their parents. In a society where wealthy men often had multiple wives, we only know of one wife for Job. He certainly could have afforded more but he only had one. Are some of these issues why God thinks highly of Job?

So, God and Satan enter into a bet. God bets Job will still honor God if he hits trouble. Satan bets Job will curse God if Job no longer has a protected and good life. Satan takes everything from Job except a few servants and Job's wife. Job is devastated. He tears his robe and shaves his head, both signs of extreme anguish. Then he does something unexpected: at least it was unexpected by Satan. Job falls on the ground and worships God. He says something we all should remember: we came into the world with nothing and we will leave with nothing. All we have that will last is our relationship with God.

Job gives us a wonderful example of how we should handle difficulty. We should worship. I know for a fact that worship changes when life is tough. We don't always feel like singing our worship or reading the Bible. But we need to worship the best we know how and continue to be obedient to the God who gave us life and entrusted us with difficulty. God is in the process of perfecting us. Our response should be to continue to worship in the midst of difficulty.

God knows what we need

Job 2:1-10

Since Satan could not get Job to curse God by taking all his possessions away, Satan asks for permission to take Job's health. I believe it is important to know that Satan can only do what God allows. That often doesn't make handling difficulties any easier but we need to remember that God is still in control. Job loses his health and he develops painful sores all over his body. It sounds like he had no way to get comfortable. (There weren't any foam mattresses back then.) Instead, Job sits in ashes and scrapes the puss off his body so it won't get hard and hurt.

I worked for several years at, and now serve on the Board of Directors for, a Christ-centered, non-profit, childcare agency. Sometimes at the beginning of our Board of Directors meetings, before we actually conduct business, we have children staying at the agency share their stories with us. One meeting, a normal looking, pretty young lady attended and shared her story with the Board. She started by showing pictures of what she looked like when she first came to campus. She was a meth amphetamine addict and her body was covered with large sores. It was ugly and looked really painful. I'm guessing this is similar to what Job looked like.

In the midst of this suffering, Job's wife finally speaks. She encourages Job to curse God and die. I have often wondered what her motivation was. Was she just mad at God? Probably. Was she only thinking about herself? She had probably been living in extreme luxury and everything had been taken away from her, too. Her own husband couldn't really care for her. She couldn't divorce him and remarry but, if he died, she could remarry. With all the wealth Job had before Satan took it, she probably had the luxury of making and keeping herself beautiful. She probably could find another husband.

Or was she just being compassionate? Here was the "greatest man among all the people of the East" who was now a nobody. He was in great suffering. He had lost everything. Perhaps she thought he would be better off dead and basically told him this. No matter what her motivation, Job's reply is amazing. He asks, "Shall we accept good from God, and not trouble?" Great question.

Why is it we are so happy and thank God when things are going well for us and then turn our backs on God when things are difficult? Why is it we trust God when things are good and no longer trust God when things are difficult? If God is God, He knows what he is doing. Should we face God and praise Him when things are going well but curse Him when things are not going well? Of course not! Job knew this. Job knew that, in this life, we have both good and trouble. Our role is to accept both good and trouble. Our role is to live out a faithful example in the midst of good times and hardship (trouble). Wealth and difficulties are both motivators to turn our back on God. In the midst of extreme wealth, Job worshipped God. In the midst of extreme difficulties, Job worshipped God. We should do the same.

Offering our presence

Job 2:11-13

Three of Job's friends learn about Job's difficulties and visit him. When they get close, they begin to realize how bad Job's plight was. Job was in such bad shape that they "could hardly recognize him".

When I was 16, a family from our church asked me to help drive the mom and daughter to a different state to join the rest of the family. For some reason, the rest of the family had traveled ahead and I was asked to help drive around Chicago. I'm not sure why they thought I was capable of doing that type of driving when I was so young but I was happy to go because this gave me the opportunity to visit with one of my best friends for an entire week who had moved to this state. It was a good week. On the way back home, the dad suggested we stop in Chicago and visit Don.

Don was about 5 years older than me and I had known him my entire life as we went to church together. The summer before, Don and some friends had been at a beach on Lake Michigan. When it was time to leave, Don dove into the water to wash off all the sunscreen but he dove in too steeply, hit his head on the bottom, and didn't come up. His friends finally realized this, found him underwater, and got him to the surface before he drowned. But he had broken his neck and was in the hospital hoping to regain the use of his arms and legs. It wasn't looking hopeful.

When we walked into the room where the nursing station told us Don was staying, I saw two people but I didn't see Don. Then someone spoke and asked if someone was there. It was Don's voice. At that moment, I realized just how great his suffering was. Don had been a handsome, buff, young man, but the man before me was wasted away. He had almost no muscle, had a halo around his head with screws going into his skull, and was stretched out on a bed. It was Don but not the Don I knew. This must have been similar to what Job's friends experienced when they saw Job. It was Job but not the same Job they had known. Job's friends just sat there with Job. They didn't talk, they were just there with him. I believe this is a great example of how to be with people who are suffering. Just be there. Don't talk. Just be with them.

Years ago when I was much younger, the wife of an elder in our church decided she wasn't being treated well and started to openly have an affair with another man. I had experienced some tension with the husband over the years and didn't believe he was always fair either. But I knew he needed someone and so I began calling him and listening. Every week I called and asked how he was doing. He began to talk and I would just listen. Sometimes he talked a long time. I don't believe I ever gave advice because I didn't know what to say anyway. The situation ended well and the couple got back together. They came before the church and asked for reconciliation. People went forward to hug them and offer forgiveness. When I got to them, they held onto me and expressed how much I had meant to them. Honestly, I didn't think I had done much. All I had done was call and listen. Maybe when people are suffering, just being there is what matters most. When we try to give advice, it usually isn't what the person needs anyway. They just need us to be there. It is probably the best we can give.

God is perfecting us

Job 3:1-26

Starting in Chapter 3, Job begins talking. To this point, it seems Job has handled his suffering pretty well. But in Chapter 3, he "curses the day of his birth". He makes it pretty obvious that he now wishes he had never been born. In verse 25 he even says he had feared and dreaded this type of thing happening to him. We start to get a picture into Job's heart. Severe suffering does this to and for us: it gives us a picture of what is in our heart. We see in Chapters 1 and 2 that God thought pretty highly of Job. Obviously, God doesn't expect us to already be perfect.

I'm not perfect. While I have always known of my imperfection, one area was pointed out pretty clearly to me when Rebecca was alive. Rebecca spent the first two months of her life at Riley Children's Hospital. After we brought her home for the first time, we started going through cycles of health and illness. These cycles became frustratingly predictable. We would be at Riley and the doctors would discharge Rebecca. Riley is a good hospital and often totally full. When a patient is barely good enough to go home, they go home so another child can have the bed. When Rebecca was good enough to go home, we would be sent home.

But once we got home, Rebecca would have problems. It could be a fever, vomiting, or something else but it would keep us up all night. We would call the doctor assigned to her and be given advice. By morning when nothing was helping, the doctor would tell us to bring her back. After a couple of these situations, I knew what was going to happen when I got to Riley and I would start to become angry. I would take Rebecca back by myself because we still had 4 other kids at home and my wife had been up all night, too, and she was exhausted. I would drive the 100+ miles to the hospital, check in at triage (the emergency room), and wait. Sometimes the wait was several hours before they actually gave you a room in ER.

Then the explaining would begin. Riley is a teaching hospital so the first doctor to visit was a resident. I would explain what was going on to the resident. Then a fellow would come into the room. Fellows are doctors who are still receiving more training so they are just past the resident stage. After the fellow, the real doctor would come in. It could be several hours between doctors but wasn't usually that long. After explaining the symptoms to all of these doctors, they would try to find us a room. One time, we stayed in ER all night until a room opened up.

When they had a room for us on a floor, we would go there and the explaining would start all over again. Depending on the symptoms, there could be a resident, fellow, and doctor from two or more specialties who wanted to know what was happening. It was usually late at night before I got to lay down somewhere and it was too late to get a room at Ronald McDonald House. I had been up for at least 36 hours, was dead tired and angry. In the midst of this, God started talking to me about my anger and how I wasn't a very patient person.

Many years after Rebecca died, we were on a road trip out west and my mom was along. My mom had never seen the west, my dad had died a few years earlier, and it seemed like a good idea to invite her to go with us. The trip was three full weeks and I was the only male with five females. It was my wife and me, my mom, and our three youngest daughters. While it went well, mornings could be a bit more tense. My mom and I are generally morning people but the rest of the family took some time to get around. One morning my mom and I were in the van waiting on the others and my mom commented on how patient I was. I had never thought of myself as being patient but then it struck me that I probably was more patient than how I had been when Rebecca was alive. God had used Rebecca's life to help me learn to deal with my anger and become a more patient person. I believe this is often the case. God wants to use our suffering to change us. We need to work with Him.

Embracing Hardship

Psalm 139: 1-12

In the first part of Psalm 139, David talks about the greatness of God. In essence, David says there is no place he can go where God is not present. God is everywhere. There is no place to hide from God. If this is really true (and I believe it is true), then why are we tempted to run and hide from God when life gets tough? So often, I have seen people want to get as far away from God as possible when they believe life is no longer fair. Life isn't fair. But that doesn't mean it is God's fault.

David is saying that God knows all about me. God even knows what I am going to say before I say it and that ability is just more than David could really comprehend. I agree with David. Somehow, my God is big enough that He has abilities I can't understand. I believe it is true that God knows what is going to happen before it happens but I don't quite understand that. Maybe it is like C.S. Lewis suggests that history is like a book and God has the ability to be anywhere in the book at any time. I don't know for sure but that could be true. At least I can understand how I can be anywhere in a book I want to be.

So, if God is so great, and, again, I believe He is, why would I ever try to run from Him? Why would I ever want to get away? The best place to be when life is hard is as close to God as possible. If He is so powerful, I would want to be very close to that powerful being. I suppose trying to get away is the mindset that God doesn't really care or love us. We choose to not believe Romans 8 where Paul states that God works in all things for our good. If we don't believe that, we may try to get away from God - which David says is impossible. We may become like Job's wife and be angry at God. We may want to just curse God and die.

I believe God is big enough to handle our anger. If you happen to be angry at God just tell Him! Relationships deepen when there is total honesty. The same thing works in marriage. We were told by our case manager at Riley Children's Hospital that over 80% of dads leave the family when there is a child with heart issues. Rebecca had a 3 chambered heart so there were definitely heart issues. I guess dads either can't handle the stress of a child that sick or just don't like the lack of freedom a sick child can bring. Maybe it is some of both. But most of them leave the family and put the responsibility to care for the child on the mom. In all honesty, my marriage got a lot better while Rebecca was alive. I'm not trying to be super spiritual because I'm not. But both my wife and me decided we really needed each other to make it through that time in life and we grew closer. It was still really hard and I know a lot of people were praying for us but we made the choice to get closer.

Hang onto God when times get tough. Pursue God. Devotedly pursue God. Worship God during your difficulties. Get as close as possible. You can't hide from God anyway.

We have value!

Psalm 139: 13-18

After David discusses how God is everywhere, he talks about how God created us. God knows us before we are born. Our beings are "fearfully and wonderfully made". God knows all about us before we live out our lives. This seems to fit God's ability to be anywhere in the book at any point in time. David even says all our days are written in God's book before we live them out.

Then in verses 17 and 18, David reveals how God thinks about us! In the NIV, verse 17 is translated "How precious to me are your thoughts, God!" But there is a footnote stating this could be translated "precious are your thoughts concerning me". When we read verse 18 about counting the thoughts, the second translation makes more sense than the first. How could we ever count God's thoughts? That would be impossible. So the translation where God thinks about us is the one that I think fits best. In any case, David is saying the God thinks about me! God's thoughts about me are precious. God cares about me! I have value!

We all know that, at times, we don't feel very valuable. We look at the people around us and think about how skilled they are compared to us and we can get depressed. That happened to me in my doctoral program. There were some amazingly smart people in my cohort and the other cohorts I had classes with. They could process information way faster than I could process information. They remembered things way better than I could remember things. It didn't take me long to realize that they were just way smarter than I am. At first, I felt inferior. I knew I would never be as smart as they were. Then it hit me, this wasn't my fault. I had never abused my mind with alcohol, drugs, or other products. I was created this way. By even attempting a doctoral program I was probably using my abilities beyond what anyone expected of me – except God. God had a purpose for me being in a doctoral program. While I don't have all that figured out yet, parts are starting to come together for me.

We all have value and a purpose. When we get fixated on those around us, we can lose sight of that purpose and value. When we keep our eyes on God, realize He continually thinks about us, and keep living out what we understand to be our own purpose to the best of our ability, we stop feeling inferior and start seeing ourselves the way God intended.

By human standards, our daughter Rebecca had little value. She never progressed past the infant stage of development. She never talked, walked, ate on her own, and we don't know if she ever heard or had any sight. But her life has impacted thousands of people over the years. Many people were impacted when she was alive. But hundreds more have been impacted in the years after she died. She lives through the devotionals I do in classes about things I learned through her life and death. Many students comment on how these devotional have really helped them as they struggle with life. One little girl, thought of as a burden to society by many, has become a blessing to hundreds of people who never met her. Doesn't that sound like something our God could accomplish?

God Provides

Psalm 24:1

It was November 1996. I was in a faculty meeting when a secretary came into the meeting to tell me I had a phone call from my wife. It turned out that my wife, who was pregnant with Rebecca, and was heading to her doctor for an appointment had gotten in a car accident. All four of our children were with her in the station wagon because we homeschooled. It was icy that day and, as she approached an embanked railroad, she started sliding and went off the embankment rolling the car a couple of times in the process. There were glass canning jars in the back of the station wagon which went flying around and breaking. The car landed upside down. The windshield was crushed. It was a total loss. Incredibly the only physical injury was that my oldest son had a small cut from flying glass.

The only other car we had was a Honda Civic. Four kids, pregnant wife, Honda Civic. Not a great transportation situation. I had started teaching college about two years earlier taking about a 70% pay cut and we didn't have much money. On top of that, I had failed to put comprehensive and collision coverages back on the station wagon when I left my corporate job and went to education. Our habit had been to only cover the vehicle which was worth the most. The station wagon had about 175,000 miles on it. We had no insurance for that car.

We started looking for a larger vehicle. We would soon have five kids so it either had to be a larger station wagon with a 3rd seat or a van. We found a station wagon that fit what we thought we would need. The asking price was $3,000; we had $2,500 saved.

The Sunday before we went to look at the car, a man from our church approached me and said he believed God wanted him to give us $500 to help buy a car. I was sure we would be able to talk the owner of the car we were going to see down on the price so I said something really stupid and prideful, "I don't think we need the money." I was wrong. We saw the car, liked it enough to buy it, and offered $2,500. The owner said he had it already priced low and needed $3,000 for the car. I went back to the man at church and told him we needed the $500. God provides.

It is now the summer of 1999. Rebecca has just died. We have one large van and no other vehicle. At home one evening, my old boss from my corporate job calls. That wasn't unusual as we would talk every few months. After talking for a while, he tells me he believes God wants him to give us money to buy a car. My pride kicks in and I tell him I think we are fine with the van we have. He says to let him know if I change my mind and we hang up.

So, I ran the numbers. I made a spreadsheet showing the cost of operating only one vehicle, the van, and what it would cost us each year if we had the van and a smaller car that got better gas mileage. You can probably guess this but operating two vehicles was actually cheaper than operating one. That might not make logical sense at first, however, gas is a huge cost of driving and, even with the extra insurance and licensing each year, it was still less money overall to drive two cars when one was a smaller car. I called my old boss back and he sent us a check to buy another car. That car lasted for about 15 years and had over 220,000 miles on it when it left our family. God provides.

Psalm 24 says that God owns it all. He is independently wealthy. But He sometimes uses other people to meet our needs. I have learned to really listen when someone tells me they have heard something from God. Most of the time, they are right.

God uses us when we are young

I Timothy 4:12

My wife and I were having lunch in the Riley Children's Hospital cafeteria one day while visiting Rebecca. As I looked out over the cafeteria, I saw two young ladies eating and told my wife that I thought one of them was a student at Grace College but I wasn't sure. The two young ladies finished eating and then stopped at our table and asked if we were the Stichter. One of them, Amy, was a student at Grace and both of them were at some training at Riley for the day. We chatted for a few minutes and then invited them up to Rebecca's room when they were done with their training.

A few hours later, they actually showed up. This was impressive because being on the ICU can be a traumatic experience. They stayed for about half an hour and then left. I thought that was pretty cool: a young person actually willing to engage in our difficult life.

About a week later, I got a phone call. The young man on the other end said he was Amy's husband, Paul. He said they had been praying about how they could help us and kept sensing maybe they could help us with vehicles. He asked if we needed a car. What a question! Actually, we were back to only one car. The summer of 1998, our Honda Civic broke down and the engine was ruined. We gave the car to a neighbor who replaced the engine and used it for several more years but we had decided to live with one vehicle. Paul said they had no kids, were both taking classes from Grace College, had three cars and, obviously, didn't need all three. We could drive the car as long as we needed it. We just needed to put gas in it and they would pay for the insurance, repairs, etc.

We didn't turn it down. We drove that car until Rebecca died on May 19, 1999. It was a tremendous blessing to us as my wife headed to Riley a couple of times a week and I needed to go to work every day. We lived close to work but when my wife was in Indianapolis, our lives were more complicated with no car. In late May or early

42

June, we gave the car back. It was only a couple of weeks later that my former boss from my previous corporate job called me and told me God was asking him to give us money to buy a car.

Paul and Amy helped us in another way, too. The large station wagon we bought just wasn't the right type of vehicle when we finally brought Rebecca home in October 1998. Rebecca had spent about 9 months in the hospital without being home and she was on a lot more machines than what she was before she left home. The hospital staff told us we really needed a van so we started looking for a van. We didn't have much money and, for the first time in about 15 years, we were looking at borrowing to buy a vehicle.

Paul and Amy heard about this and decided to help. Paul was the youth pastor at a church and convinced the youth group to raise money to help us buy a van. It was the year that Tickle Me Elmo was so popular and really hard to find. The youth group found one, auctioned it off on the radio as a fundraiser and gave us the money. Over $3,000! Our own church took up an offering and got a matching grant to help us. My brother's church donated their annual auction money to us. One of my former students gave us some money. When all the money was put together, we paid about $13 of our own money for the van!

God uses young people. Sometimes in a college setting I believe I Timothy 4:12 is overused but it is true. Young people can help when there are needs. It comes down to asking God what you can do and listening to the answer. Then stepping out in faith that you have heard correctly. When Paul called me, he was just going on what he thought God was saying. You can do the same.

Listening to God

I was 29 years old when my income took a big jump. It happens to a lot of us: the time when we get the promotion and pay increase that gives us a lot more money than we had before. Having lived in Belize, a developing country, for about three months during college, I knew I wanted to live a modest lifestyle and help those less fortunate. So my wife and I agreed we would give 20% of our gross income away and 50% of the gross amount of any bonus away. We just didn't need to increase our standard of living that much when other people had needs.

The first couple of years that I was corporate controller, I was on a temporary bonus plan. The bonuses were pretty large and we gave 50% of that money away. But that bonus plan changed and I was no longer on a bonus system. My boss was an owner of the company and he didn't like that I was not included in the bonus plan. So, every so often, he would write me a personal check to compensate for my lack of bonuses. I never asked for this, but he was a generous man. We gave 50% of the money away to help others.

One day, my boss called me into his office and closed the door. He ranted for a few minutes about how it wasn't fair that I was not on the bonus plan and then handed me a check for $3,000. I was thankful. I went home that night and showed it to my wife. We immediately knew something was different about this check. We weren't to give 50% of it away. We didn't know why so we put it in the bank and waited.

Several months later we received a letter from one of my wife's cousins who had taken his family to a foreign country to teach missionary children. For some reason, their assignment was ending and they needed to come home to the States. Since this was an unplanned return trip, they didn't have the money to return. The cost of tickets to fly back home was $3,000. We sent them the money.

Even nearly 30 years later, I think this is really cool. But it is only cool because we didn't just follow our normal operating procedure for bonuses. We were willing to listen to God and consider that God may want to do something different this time. We didn't know what that was going to be so we waited. We had to be patient and trust that God would reveal what we needed to know at the time we needed it. And He did.

I tell my students that if they will be obedient to God, even when it doesn't make a lot of sense, they will have some really cool stories to tell their grandchildren. God owns everything. But He often uses us to dispense His resources. If we aren't willing and obedient, He finds someone else who will be obedient. When we just follow our standard plan for life and aren't open to God changing our direction, we miss out.

Caught in the gravity wagon

Romans 6:11-18

We lived on a farm until I was seven years old. My dad was a full-time farmer and my mom was a farmer's wife. That meant my two brothers and I were constantly outside and immersed in the farming culture. We were a full-service farm except we didn't milk cows. But I remember sheep, pigs, chickens, feeding cattle for butcher, and raising crops. Since we lived in Indiana, most of our crops were corn and soybeans.

When it came time to harvest, my dad ran the combine and my mom unloaded wagons. We used gravity wagons. Gravity wagons have tall sides with three of the sides starting to slant toward the fourth side closer to the bottom of the wagon. This allows grain to slide out of the wagon only due to gravity and with no effort. All you had to do was slide up the door at the bottom of the wagon and grain would run out the open door.

When my mom didn't have anyone to watch us young boys, we went with her. I remember climbing up on top of the gravity wagons and playing in the grain as mom got ready to unload them. Since the grain wasn't allowed to run out very fast or it would clog up the grain auger used to lift the grain to the top of the storage bins, we could be up in the wagon for awhile and stay out of the way. I'm not sure whether our mom knew this but we liked to allow our feet to be sucked down into the grain as it slowly exited the wagon and then we would pull ourselves up out of the grain before we got sucked in too far. If we kept ahold of the side of the wagon, we could pull ourselves out.

I was the middle child with a brother one year older and a brother about 2 ½ years younger. I'm guessing I was 5 or 6 when the following event occurred, making my younger brother about 3 years old at the time. My younger brother let himself get sucked in too far and lost his grip on the side of the wagon. My older brother and I tried to pull him up out of the grain but he was too far in. We yelled at our mom to let her know but before she could shut the door, my brother's head was under the grain. We were all frantic. My mom couldn't pull him out either. So she did the only thing that could save him, she shut off the auger, opened the door all the way, let the grain fall on the ground, and he came out the open door feet first. He is still a pretty smart guy today so I don't think there was any permanent damage.

Sometimes we have to hit bottom to find our way out. We like to play in sin thinking we can always get out. Pornography can be like this. I know a man who dabbled in porn thinking he could get out. His wife found out and continued to warn him but he kept watching porn. Ultimately, he got in too far, Satan had a very strong hold on him, and he hit bottom. He had to get help. He is doing well today but he played around with sin and it sucked him in. Sometimes we need to let go and get help to find out way out. We all struggle at times but Satan tries to convince us that no one will care and that we are all alone. This just isn't true! If you are caught in sin, let go and get help. Start by just admitting you need help to someone you trust. Just let go! It will be the beginning of getting out.

Devotionals given in Intermediate Accounting I

This series of devotionals utilized I Thessalonians as the scripture guiding us how to live among people who don't know Christ Jesus. Paul lived and worked among the Thessalonians and, when he wrote this letter to them, Paul talked about the concepts he was trying to live among them. Since most Accounting majors will start working a job among people who have no concept of God or, at least, have no desire to please God, the concepts Paul discusses in I Thessalonians are a good study on why we learn a profession and live in the world.

THUSEM

I Thessalonians 1:1-5

Paul starts out his first book to the Thessalonian church in his usual manner. He greats them, offers grace and peace, and tells them how he is thankful for them. He then mentions faith, hope, and love in a little different order than are in I Corinthians 13 but with a similar message.

Paul was certain the Thessalonian believers were staying true to their faith because the gospel was being displayed with power, with the Holy Spirit, and with deep conviction in their midst. It seems this is one way to know when the gospel has really taken hold in a community of believers.

The second part of verse 5 is powerful. It states that Paul and his helpers lived among the Thessalonian believers for their (the Thessalonian's) sake. Notice that Paul didn't say they were living among the Thessalonians for their own (Paul's) sake. It was for the sake of the Thessalonians.

I believe this is the essence of why Christians aren't whisked away once they come to saving faith. It is so we are able to live among those who either don't yet know God or who need some help figuring out how to live in a way that is pleasing to God. We live in the world for the sake of the world. THUSEM – US in the midst of THEM. We live in the world for the sake of the world.

Accounting majors don't just study accounting during college so they have a better chance to get a great job and pass the CPA exam. They study accounting so they have a way to get into the world of other accountants and make an impact for Jesus. How else would believers be able to get into a world where money seems to be the most important thing to think about all day and accumulate so much of it? It's not so that you can spend the rest of a meaningless life having fun before you die. Accounting is an avenue to reach other accountants who need a savior. Studying marketing during college is a way to reach people who need a savior. Studying education is the same. Choose any college major and it should be the same goal.

So often we miss the big picture of why we are learning. Certainly one reason is so we can support ourselves and not be dependent on others to pay our way in life. But the big reason is so we have a way to get among THEM. Us living in the midst of them. Isn't that what Jesus did for us? He came to earth for us, not for him. He came to live among us to teach us what was pleasing to God. In the same way we learn and, later, live for the sake of THEM.

Who are you Imitating?

I Thessalonians 1:6-10

After Paul told the Thessalonian believers that he had been living among them for their sake, he commended them for imitating him. Apparently there was some suffering that accompanied the Thessalonians accepting the gospel message and Paul was acquainted with suffering! He had been shipwrecked, whipped, and jailed. But he persevered and he must have become quite a good example to others when they faced persecutions. If Paul could endure so much for the sake of the gospel, they could also endure some suffering or even "severe suffering" as mentioned in verse 6.

Then Paul goes on to tell the Thessalonians that they had become a model to other believers. The Thessalonians might not have known this and it had to be encouraging to them to realize that, just as they had imitated Paul, others were now imitating them. Paul even says that their faith was becoming known everywhere! That must have really been encouraging to the Thessalonians.

Who are you imitating? I believe we all imitate. We learn by imitating. One of the benefits of having children and raising them is that we find out so much about ourselves. I remember when my young sons would do or say something and it would hit me that they had just imitated me. Sometimes I wasn't very happy about what I saw or heard. Some of the things I did and said weren't things I wanted them to imitate. I began to pay more attention to my words and actions. I believe that God uses our own children to initiate change in us. So, are you imitating people who will make you better or do you find yourself imitating people you wouldn't want your children to imitate?

Paul then says that the Thessalonians' faith is becoming known everywhere. Is your faith becoming known broadly? When people come in contact with you do they leave knowing you are a person of faith? If you don't think so, maybe you are imitating the wrong people. I believe one of the reasons God keeps us on this earth is so others have someone to imitate. As I get older, I think about this more. I want to finish my life strong, not as so many Old Testament characters finished. We have so many examples in the Old Testament of people who didn't finish well.

I encourage us to seriously think about who we imitate and whether our lives are a good model for others to imitate. When we choose well, our faith will start to become known everywhere.

Who am I trying to please?

I Thessalonians 2:1-6

In these verses, Paul states a couple of issues with which I constantly battle. In verse 4, Paul makes sure the Thessalonians know that, when he was with them, he was trying to please God, not people. I like being a people-pleaser. I want people to like me and, if given the choice, will act in ways that I believe help people to like me. This isn't all bad as it often means I treat others in a way I would also want to be treated. Most of the time, that is a good policy.

But I can do this without thinking about whether what I am doing is pleasing to God. If a student is not doing well in my class and I am aware of outside issues they could control which could help them improve their performance, then I am faced with a choice of whether or not to confront the student. Confronting them might not please them; therefore, I don't want to confront them because I want them to like me. But that might be totally contrary to what would please God. I had a recent student who was overextended evidenced by their missing deadlines and not communicating well with me about the issues. I wanted to just let it slide because the student would be graduating soon and I didn't want her to not like me when she left college.

After a lot of thought, I decided to write her an email and point out the issues because I knew it was more important for her future that she have the opportunity correct the issue. I even wrote that I hoped she didn't hate me for saying what I said. She replied pretty quickly thanking me for saying what I did and stating that "of course I don't hate you". I'm not saying I will receive that type of response every time but it encouraged me to appropriately address issues instead of shying away from them out of fear that someone may not like me for doing so.

Paul says something else in the first part of verse 6 that ties in pretty well. He says they were not looking for praise from any person.

Again, I struggle with this. I like to be praised by people. When I was using this devotional in class one day, a student asked me if that was why I handed out pieces of paper a couple of times per semester and asked students for feedback. I think it was a pretty good question. I had to ponder that and, if being honest with myself, it was part of the reason. I like getting praise from students. I really did want to know how I could improve the class and if there was something I was missing but I really, really liked reading good things about me.

Wanting to be continually praised is a sure sign of a misguided heart. I should be looking to God for praise, not people. I should be doing things and acting in ways which please God not doing things so I can get praise from people. I need to do the right things because I know that is what God wants me to do even if no person praises me.

Who are you trying to please? To whom do you look for praise?

Work hard and share your life

I Thessalonians 2:7-9

In these verses, Paul says they worked hard when they were with the Thessalonians so they wouldn't be a burden to the Thessalonians while they shared life together. I believe working hard is a prerequisite for sharing your faith.

As is pointed out in chapter 1, we live among people so we can draw them to Christ – THUSEM. But they won't listen to us if they don't respect us. The business world is a fast-moving place. To be excellent in the world of business, most of us really need to work hard. If you aren't willing to work hard, you won't be respected. Sometime this means we need to put in longer hours but not always. So much time can be lost getting distracted by social media or emails that we don't really get as much work done in 8 hours as we ought. Then we need to work more hours to make up for the time that was wasted.

I tell students that working hard is not the same thing as working long hours. If they will refrain from social media during work hours, personal email or texts, and other distractions, they will be able to get more work done in a shorter timeframe than most other people in the office. People will notice and respect them. I believe it is nearly impossible to get a chance to speak into people's lives about Christ if we aren't respected. Not working hard is almost a sure bet that we won't be listened to when we try to share Christ.

But working hard and doing good work has the opposite effect. It will open doors for us to talk. Oftentimes people will be the most open when work is over and we are with them in a social setting. But if we never go with them to share life, we won't get this chance. I don't believe I did this well during my early career. I had been taught that going to bars was bad and I didn't want to get caught there, so I just didn't go. Now, I wish I would have gone. I still don't drink alcohol but I could have still gone along and talked with them.

Because of this, I didn't get to share my life as much as I wish I would have.

Paul, on the other hand, shared life with the Thessalonians. He worked hard and shared his life. I believe these go together well and Paul knew that. If he had been a freeloader, asking for them to support him (or do the work he didn't have time to do because he was wasting time at the office), the Thessalonians would not have been nearly as open to listening to the gospel. I encourage you to work hard and share your life.

Holy, righteous, blameless

I Thessalonians 2:10-12

In these three verses, Paul states that he and his companions lived holy, righteous, and blameless lives when they spent time with the Thessalonians. I don't know about you but I doubt there has been a time in my life where I was perfectly this way for a very long time. Then Paul states that he was like a father to the Thessalonians by encouraging, comforting, and urging them to live lives worthy of God (v 12). Again, I have struggled to have this type of perspective when I was among people who did not yet fully grasp God's salvation.

So often, especially when I am hurt by someone who is not a believer, I don't even come close to living in a way that is holy, righteous, or blameless. There was one time during my life when I believed I was taken advantage of by another employee who was older and higher ranking than I was and it just wasn't fair. While the owners of the business made sure I realized they didn't feel the same way about me and tried to encourage me, I just couldn't let it go. It was a classic case of unforgiveness on my part. In the end, it hurt my Christian witness and it hurt me. When I was finally able to forgive, I needed to go to a couple of people, confess my attitude issues, and make it right.

I believe Paul was able to live in a different mindset than what I was living. He realized that people who don't yet have a full comprehension of how God wishes them to live will be living for themselves and that means they will, sometimes, hurt other people intentionally. Whether it is to get ahead in life or just be mean, it will happen. I think Paul's instruction is that we are to still live among others (THUSEM) in a way that is holy, righteous, and blameless. Our attitude must be that we encourage, comfort, and urge others to live in a way that pleases (is worthy of) God. This means we will need to have a tough skin sometimes and be ready to forgive quickly. It doesn't mean we condone poor behavior because poor behavior isn't pleasing to God. But it does mean we have to look beyond such behavior and instruct others on what pleases God. Isn't this what a good father does when dealing with his own children? He knows they won't always be perfect but he must instruct in the midst of imperfect behavior.

I believe I have grown from when I wasn't able to forgive quickly. I still address behavior which isn't pleasing to God. But it means I don't allow such behavior to cause me to behave in ways equally unpleasing to God. I try to instruct others what it would mean to behave in holy, righteous, and blameless ways.

Hope, joy, and crown

I Thessalonians 2: 17-20

The last few verses of chapter 2 give us a pretty clear picture of what should bring us joy. In the United States, we have so many things that fight for our loyalty and promise to bring us joy. For people who are through basic education, it is often our work or trying to get that next promotion. For some, it is the next thing we want to buy. For many young people, it is getting more social media attention whether it is "likes" or the number of other people following us. These things can consume our thinking and give us a reason to live. They can also lead us into depression and into feeling like we don't want to live.

Paul says something different. It is people who were his hope, joy, and crown. I believe this is exactly what God intended. It is to be people who give us a reason for living. Let's be honest, why else would we really want to stay on this earth. If we believe scripture, the next life outside the confines of our physical body is much better. No more getting old and the frustrations that come with it. My body doesn't feel as good as it used to feel. It is wearing out. I often feel confined by my body and I'm a pretty healthy person. But someday, I will not be confined by this body. Why would I want to stay in it? People! It is people.

Paul knew that people and the effect he could have on them was a reason to go on living well. While we know that people bring us frustration and we can be frustrating to others, people also bring us joy and we can bring joy to others. Our hope should be that, by living our lives well and encouraging others to live their lives well, we lead them to salvation. I have often wondered if the crowns we receive, as mentioned in Revelation, are the result of people. Maybe they are people. The people we have influenced for Christ. While I don't know for sure, this makes a lot of sense and Paul seems to support this in these verses.

People are our hope, joy, and crown. In a world that tells us our hope, joy, and reward should be built on more money, more prestige, more likes, or more followers, Paul says it is people. People aren't always my focus but need to be more of my focus. Spending time with people should be a high priority for me. Spending time with people should be a high priority for you. It was for Paul and, if I read the Gospels correctly, it was for Jesus.

Such Great Love

I Thessalonians 3:1-13

Chapter 3 seems to be about love. The first five verses relay how Paul was so concerned for the Thessalonians that he was willing to send someone to find out how they were doing. Paul knew the Thessalonians were facing trials and persecution and he wondered if their faith was staying strong in the midst of these trials. Remember, Paul had worked hard when he was with the Thessalonians to model what a walk with Christ should look like and now he was concerned these trials and persecutions had caused the Thessalonians to give up their faith.

But Timothy found a thriving church and reported some pretty good things back to Paul. Not only was the Thessalonian church doing a good job of loving, they had maintained their great faith. Sometimes we call this the divine perpendicular. Loving is an act carried out to each other or a parallel act. Faith is a perpendicular act reaching "upward" to God. When those two lines are put together, they create a cross. Isn't this exactly what Jesus came to teach? Love God, love people? The Thessalonians were doing exactly this.

As I read the rest of Chapter 3, I get the feeling like this wording is something I would use about my own children. I have seven living children, three children in-law, and one child, Rebecca, who died after spending most of her 26 months of life in the hospital. All of my children are living out a Christian life. It brings me great joy. That wasn't always the case as there were times when one or more of my children were struggling in their faith, just as I did at one particular time during college. My wife and I prayed "most earnestly" for our children during those times and continue to pray for them. We don't just want our children to live out a Christian life but to have it deepen and flow out to people they live and work with. We want them to love God and love people in ways that draw others to Christ.

Paul wanted the same thing for the Thessalonians and it seemed to be happening.

Overall, as I read this chapter, I get a sense of the deep love Paul had for the Thessalonians. I often ask myself whether I had the same type of love for the people I live and work with. If I'm totally honest with myself, I often don't. I get too caught up in my own life, hopes, dreams, lust for more stuff, etc. I just don't care enough for other people. I have a note stuck to my computer screen which reads, Don't be 'busy'. It is a reminder to me that, when students or other people stop by, I need to make them feel like I have time for them. While I have further to go to really achieve this all the time, I think I'm getting better. It means I will both be loving God and loving people better. I want that. Do you?

Live a Holy Life

I Thessalonians 4:1-8

After Paul has expressed his great love for the Thessalonians in chapter 3, he gives them some instructions. I have to believe he had already said these things to them many times when he lived with them but they must have been important enough to state again. As Paul states in verse 1, these instructions were of things that pleased God. Since God doesn't change, they would be things that still please God today.

The first one is to avoid sexual immorality. It seems we all have a little different idea of what constitutes sexually immoral behavior. I think Paul states something in Ephesians 5:3 that might help. In Ephesians, Paul says there should not even be a hint of sexual immorality in the ways you live. Back in Paul's time, there wasn't television or the internet so most of what would have been sexually immoral then would be the way they treated other people. Jesus was pretty clear that sinful behaviors begin with the mind. Today we need to be aware of how immoral thoughts can begin with things we watch on TV or the internet. A good question to ask is would you still be watching this if your young children were around. If not, there probably is at least a hint of immorality in what you are doing.

The second thing Paul tells the Thessalonians is they need to learn to control their own body in a way that is holy and honorable (v. 4). This fits in well with the first instruction but I believe it extends past sexual immorality. It extends to all types of lusts. Paul mentions passionate lust in verse 5. I believe I have experienced passionate lust for stuff sometimes. I want something so much that I'm constantly thinking about it and planning how to make it happen. During those times of life, I don't pay as much attention to people and concentrate on the thing or things I want. I'm a country boy at heart and, while cars don't really tempt me, trucks do. I can spent a lot of time researching pickup trucks, thinking about them, trying to justify buying a diesel pickup and, during this time, knowing it isn't something I should be doing. I'm not controlling myself well. Paul speaks to that in this passage.

The third thing Paul says is we should not wrong or take advantage of each other. It appears he is tying this into lust. When we are sharing life with each other in the church, it is easy to make really good friendships with the opposite sex. If we aren't careful, these friendships can grow into lustful thoughts and possibly affairs. Paul is telling the Thessalonians to be extremely careful because God will punish such sins. I think God punishes all sin but this type is extremely damaging to not only us, but others, too. How many families have been broken and children torn apart because someone didn't control their lust and behavior?

The fourth thing Paul reminds the Thessalonians of is that God calls us to live a holy life. Holy literally means "set apart", different: not like others in the world. By not getting caught up in lust, we are living different and the world will notice. I heard a speaker teaching on this passage summarize it by saying verses 3-8 teach us to be "decent". I think that is a good way to summarize it.

Work hard and mind your own business

I Thessalonians 4:9-12

After Paul encourages the Thessalonians to live a holy life in verse 7, he goes on to give them two good principles – work hard and mind your own business. I have worked in enough companies to know that most people will work hard when others are watching or when there is something extremely important to have done but often will not work very hard if no one is watching. I'm not talking about factory work. After graduating from college, I have always worked in "professional" settings.

Paul instructs the Thessalonians to work with their hands. I don't believe he was just saying that only working with your hands was appropriate. But he certainly was saying that the Thessalonians needed to support themselves. We see in other passages that some people could no longer support themselves and Paul gave instruction about who was worthy of support and who was not. Those who could work should work. Paul seems to say that those outside the Christian faith would respect believers who worked hard. I often tell students that they need to work hard so they gain the respect of their coworkers. If they aren't respected in their work, it will be extremely difficult to be able to share Christ. If your work isn't respected, your message won't be respected either. Paul knew this.

Just before this in verse 11, Paul says to lead a quiet life and mind your own business. This isn't the only time Paul gives this type of encouragement. In II Thessalonians, Paul has to chide the Thessalonians for not taking his advice in I Thessalonians. Some of them had become "busybodies" and were causing disruption. They weren't working hard and minding their own business. They were getting involved in other people's lives unnecessarily and causing disruption because of it. I have found that not having enough to do often leads to discontented people while being busy keeps people from complaining. I'm not talking about purposefully overworking people but about making sure you only have the employees you really need. Having too many employees gives the employees time to get too involved in things that shouldn't concern them. There needs to be a good balance at work.

I believe God created us for meaningful labor. When we don't have meaningful things to do, we get bored and don't live a fruitful life. Look at how many extremely wealthy people are depressed and how quickly some retired people die while other retired people live a long time. Often it is those retired people who fill their time still doing meaningful things who live longer. Work hard and mind your own business. It is good advice.

Stay Awake

I Thessalonians 5:1-11

Christ's return is getting closer. Just the fact that time is moving on means we are getting closer to Christ's return. Jesus said that when the world becomes more disrupted, it is just the beginning of "birth pains". I like math puzzles and have wondered how long it really is from the beginning of birth pains until delivery. Depending on the pregnancy, it could be a month, a couple of weeks, or it all happens in one day. If we assume the pregnancy began when Christ left the earth, we have had about 2,000 years of pregnancy so far. If the beginning of birth pains was a month before delivery, we have about 180 years (or approximately one-ninth of the total time) from the beginning of wars, earthquakes, and famines until Christ's return. If it is two weeks, we have about 100 years. If it is the same day, we have less than 10 years. I'm not trying to predict anything because Jesus also said we wouldn't know the exact time and none of us really knows when the birth pains began.

But Paul says we should not be surprised by Christ's return. Paul relates Christ's return to a thief. Thieves steal valuable things and they don't announce when they are coming. They usually come when there is darkness. It is a surprise. Paul is telling the Thessalonians that Christ's return should not be a surprise to them. They need to be aware of the signs and be prepared. They need to examine their hearts and determine if Christ's coming will seem like a thief's coming to them. For believers, Christ doesn't steal anything of value. If it feels like that, we are putting too much value in things of this world.

From what Paul says in verse 3, it appears the end will come in a time when there is relative peace and people feel relatively safe. Will this be a prosperous economic time? Will it be when the terrorist activity we now face has been relatively tamed? I guess we don't know for sure.

Paul makes it clear that the Thessalonians (and I believe this is a message for all of us) should not be stumbling around like drunk people or drowsy people. We need to stay alert! We need to be sober! In verse 11, Paul says we need to encourage each other to stay alert. He didn't want any of them to be caught asleep. We know Christ didn't return in their lifetime. But Paul continued to encourage them to live as if Christ would be returning at any time. It is a message we also need to hear. We need to be living as if Christ could return at any time. If birth pains are assumed to begin the same day as delivery, and that means less than 10 years from the beginning of the birth pains, Christ could return any day. I'm not predicting but I am encouraging you to be alert. Don't be lulled to sleep by the relative safety we enjoy in the United States. Don't be drunk by the relative prosperity we enjoy in the United States. Be awake! Be alert! Christ's return is soon. Be ready.

Some Instructions

I Thessalonians 5:12-15

In these four verses, Paul gives instruction on how we are to live together. In verse 12, Paul seems to tell them to recognize pastors who work hard. But the verse doesn't mention pastors because there probably weren't really people who functioned the way our pastors function today. But I think the ideas fit well. Not only does Paul say these people work hard but they "admonish" or warn. A good spiritual leader not only teaches but also warns. In our individualistic society, we don't always want this type of instruction. But Paul did this often in his letters and we tend to think pretty highly of Paul. Why wouldn't we want someone leading our church who is willing to admonish us when needed?

Next Paul says we are to live in peace with each other. Apparently, living in peace doesn't always mean lack of conflict. In the very next verse, Paul states the Thessalonians are to warn the idle and disruptive. Paul had previously said they were to work hard and mind their own business. Now he says they are to warn people who aren't following that previous instruction but who were causing disruption. Lack of meaningful labor often leads to disruption.

The Thessalonians were to encourage the disheartened and help the weak. They were to take care of people who weren't able to work and who were going through difficult times. They needed to be able to tell the difference between people who were lazy and those who had legitimate needs. Paul says to help these people. A good leader knows when to admonish and when to help. Some people need a good kick to get them going and some people need encouragement. But whichever is needed, Paul next says the Thessalonians needed to be patient with people.

Sometimes I struggle to be patient with people. I think they should act on my advice immediately. This isn't being patient. Sometimes people need time to think through things and decide how they will act. I don't believe this means we bail out people who could work but decide they are just going to be lazy. But it does mean we continue to love them and do what Paul says next – do what is good for each other. Sometimes what is good is giving aid. Sometimes it is giving advice. It doesn't sound like it ever means giving up.

I am on a local Habitat for Humanity board. We don't give houses away. We help build a house that the family buys from Habitat but at a zero interest rate. The family is required to help build the house, too. Families apply to be considered for a house. Sometimes the family needs to be told they need to work harder in caring for themselves. Not everyone needs help. Some people need encouragement. We need to acknowledge those among us who are gifted at telling the difference.

Rejoice, Pray, Give Thanks

I Thessalonians 5:16-18

The 19 words in these short verses pretty well sum up the way we are to live our lives. Verse 16: Rejoice always. Do you wake up each morning thanking God for life and that He has given you another day to live? I believe this is a good first step toward rejoicing always. We all know that life doesn't always mean good things happen. Paul knew this, too. Our ability to rejoice shouldn't be dependent on how good our life is at the moment. We should be rejoicing just because we have life. I think we should also rejoice because, when things are going really well, we have a promise that God is working all things to our good. We just don't have the ability to see that yet.

I'll give two examples. We have geothermal heating and cooling in our house. When we had the house built about 20 years ago, it just made economic sense to install geo. But the company who built our heating/cooling unit went out of business several years afterward, we couldn't get replacement parts, and parts were failing. So, we decided to replace the entire unit while we could still get a 30% credit off our taxes. A couple of days after the new unit was installed, I woke up one morning hearing a "shhhhhhh" sound. Not knowing what it was, I headed downstairs and stepped into water. A pipe fitting had cracked and flooded our entire basement. It was so frustrating! In the moment, I wasn't rejoicing. But after a few hours and the company who dried out the basement showed up, I told my wife that we needed to see what good came out of this. The settlement from the installer's insurance company was pretty good. We did some work ourselves and were able to not only replace things in the basement, we were able to pay to replace the entire upstairs kitchen floor, which had more than worn out, too. In the end, we rejoiced in our difficulty.

The other example was our daughter, Rebecca, who lived 26 months with about 21 of those spent in the hospital. It was an extremely difficult life for us. We had 4, and then 5, other children to care for and a daughter living 100 miles away in the hospital. Our church family was great but life was hard. After Rebecca died, we tried to piece things together. I began using her life, our struggles during it, and her death in devotionals I shared with my students. Students started saying how much these devotionals were helping them. I started getting a lot of great evaluation comments about the devotionals. Students said things like, "I don't like accounting but I love coming to class because of the devotions." While I wish all students would come to class because they just love accounting, I am glad they are coming for something. God took our difficulty and turned it into something good. I'm rejoicing.

Paul also says to pray continually. We all know this isn't physically possible so he must have meant something else. I believe this is a mindset. We need to continually have a prayer mindset. All during our days, we need to turn to God in prayer. The world tries to distract us with the internet and other distractions. But we can learn to have God on our minds all during the day. When we are able to rejoice and pray, we are able to give thanks in all circumstances. I don't believe we will always have a thankful attitude exactly when something bad happens but we will quickly turn our minds to thanking the God who cares and works out all things to our good.

The Spirit's fire

I Thessalonians 5:19-22

As final instructions to the Thessalonian church, Paul encourages them to "not put out the Spirit's fire." Paul then seems to tie this into prophecies. If the Thessalonians treated prophecies with contempt, they were potentially hindering the Holy Spirit's ability to work in their lives. Contempt is an act of despising, dishonoring, or disgracing something. I think every Christian would agree we don't want to despise, dishonor, or disgrace the Holy Spirit. But in many churches in the United States, prophecy isn't even considered. Paul tells the Thessalonians to test prophecies. If it is "good", hold on to it. If it is "harmful", reject it. So, how do we know the difference?

I believe that most of us, when we hear the word "prophecy", think of predictions of the future. In the Old Testament, prophets foretold the future but mostly they just spoke the truth for God. If Israel was not being obedient to God's desires, prophets came and told the king and/or the people that God wasn't pleased. Sometimes prophets also told what would happen if the people didn't repent.

I have some experience with prophecies. Most prophecies (when someone relays what they believe God is wanting to say) I have experienced were encouraging. The person speaking for God was giving an encouraging message to the other person. I have had some of those given to me. They are amazingly helpful. In times when I have been questioning myself or part of life, God has spoken through others in ways that have greatly encouraged me. Sometimes it was through people who knew me well. Sometimes it was through people who didn't know much about me. Most recently, it was through a friend who knew me well but hadn't experienced the part of me being spoken to. This dying man's words spoken directly to me went deep into my soul and encouraged me in ways I haven't experienced for a long time. As he spoke, it was as if God was meeting a need deep within me. It was good. I'm going to hold on to those words.

Another time wasn't as good. A person who didn't know me well but knew of a situation I was dealing with gave a prophetic word about the future. Then, he interpreted what he had said. It was encouraging at the time but the future didn't happen as he had interpreted. I was confused. If he really was speaking for God, why didn't things happen the way he said they would happen? To get help, I talked with some of the other people who were in attendance at the service where this person spoke the prophetic word. Everyone I spoke with said that when they heard the prophet's own interpretation, and "tested what he said," his interpretation did not seem right to them. It ended up being harmful to us for a while. So, we rejected that interpretation. Interestingly enough, a different interpretation emerged that fit perfectly. We continue to hold on to this interpretation. It is good and has brought us much comfort over the years.

I still believe God speaks to us through other people. We don't always call it prophecy but, when we believe God wants us to talk with someone else and encourage them, I believe that is a form of prophecy. It is speaking for God. It can be accepted by the other person or rejected by them. Most of the time, it encourages the other person. I have become bolder in speaking for God. To be clear, I don't always tell the other person that I believe God wants me to say this to them. But I hope they don't treat these words with contempt. I hope they test them and hold on to what is good. Paul knew that when we test prophecies, we much continue to connect with the Holy Spirit. It is the Holy Spirit's guidance that helps us know what is good and what is harmful. By doing this, we are not putting out the Spirit's fire.

"The Fear"

Lily Allen

One morning as I was quickly skimming the Wall Street Journal, I saw an unusual article that caught my eye. It was discussing how some musical artists were having a difficult time getting to the United States for award ceremonies. I, honestly, don't remember anymore why this was the case but, for some reason, I was interested. I now realize it was God directing me to the song, *The Fear*. I'm not a fan of British music but decided to watch a Lily Allen song on YouTube. *The Fear* was the song that came up. As I watched and listened, I heard things that fit in so well with I Thessalonians and why we are called to live among the world – THUSEM. I decided to play the video to my students and use it as a final devotional for the class.

For copyright reasons, I have not included the song in this devotional book. I encourage you to look up the lyrics. The words are honest. The song speaks of someone living without God and talking about what her life is like. She is consumed by fear but tries to calm her fear with stuff, fame, and beauty.

In her life, credit cards (plastic) are a way to consume things that take away the fear. She would do anything necessary to become famous and not be ashamed to do these things or admit the reason was to become famous. Jewels and cloths are also seen as a way to help take away fear. Of course, as Christians we can struggle with the same feelings. We struggle with consumption, fame, and beauty. But we know these things don't satisfy, so does Lily Allen. She admits in the song that she wants life to become clear.

She needs someone to model Christ to her and explain how much God wants to take this fear away. She needs someone just like you and me. We are imperfect people but we have something others need. That is why we are called to live among THEM. That is why we learn a profession during college or learn a trade in some other manner. It is so we can get into the midst of THEM and share our lives with THEM. It is so we can spend eternity with both God and THEM.

Devotionals given in Advanced Accounting

Advanced Accounting is typically the last class Accounting majors take from me. These devotionals are a combination of lessons learned as I bicycled around Michigan with my sons, as one son and I bicycled around Indiana, and during my doctoral studies. It would seem I should have learned some of these lessons earlier in life but most of these experienced happened during my 50's. I hope my students can learn these lessons earlier in their lives.

We need a Sabbath

Mark 2:23-28

After being a college professor for about 10 years, I began doctoral studies. The college asked me to get my doctorate but didn't require it. After talking with my wife and praying about it, I decided I wanted to get my doctorate. I applied to only one program with the thought that, if I didn't get in, it would be God's way of telling me not to get my doctorate. I got in and took my first classes in May 2008.

When I started doctoral studies, I was the Business Department chair, teaching ¾ time, advising about 30 students, and responsible for a lot of other aspects of a large department. I still had five children at home with two already in college. Most people would have said I was busy. I had already been working about 50 hours a week and then took on the doctorate. My workload jumped to over 60 hours a week and more than that some weeks. After a couple of years, our college implemented a "school" system and I became Dean of the School of Business.

I felt like I was constantly working because I was constantly working. While I grew up knowing practicing the Sabbath, I started disregarding the Sabbath and working Sunday afternoons and evenings as well as the other six days of the week. I wasn't at home much and my family was suffering. Finally, my wife gave me what I needed ... some really strong ultimatums about family and work. I quit the Dean position the next day and am really glad I did.

This wasn't the only time in life I had not taken a 24-hour period off each week. During college, I fell into the same routine as I had during my doctorate. I would study parts of 7 days a week and never really took time off. While being a camp counselor the summer between my junior and senior years of college, I heard some really good teaching on why we needed a Sabbath and decided to practice that my senior year.   My grades improved, I was more rested, and yet nothing about my college experience suffered, even though I was taking harder classes.

In Mark 2, we have a story about the Sabbath. God didn't create the idea of Sabbath for himself, he did it for us. We need a Sabbath. We have been created with the need for a Sabbath. Our bodies and minds need the break. When we consistently don't take the break the Sabbath affords, we suffer physically and emotionally. I don't believe doing Sabbath on Sundays is required but having a 24-hour period sometime during a week seems to be something we need.

I've done some long distance bicycling in my life actually doing a coast to coast ride the summer after graduating from college and a couple of other long, multi-day rides. I have found out the same concept with physical activity. About once every seven days, our bodies need a break. When you try to bike too many days in a row, everything suffers. God created the Sabbath for us. We need it.

Pride will be broken

Proverbs 16:18-20

The very first day of my doctoral program was orientation. We spent all afternoon in meetings where we met the others in our cohort (we started with 13 that day and 10 of us ultimately finished - which is a really good percentage for doctoral programs), met leaders of the DBA program, were given advice by these leaders, met with the cohort a year ahead of us, and had a cookout. It was a helpful afternoon.

After the @ 4 hours of orientation, we were put in a room alone with the cohort a year ahead of us. They could tell us anything they wanted without anyone from Anderson University listening in. We had half an hour together before the cookout. They started going around and telling us things they thought would help. I don't remember much of what they said anymore but two things still stand out. A couple of them said something like you will either be on your own or you will become really good friends with those in your cohort and help each other. Ultimately, we had both types of people in our cohort. I was part of a group who really helped each other. A few other people basically were on their own by their own choosing.

The second thing I remember was that several of them told us we would feel like quitting but "Don't quit!" As I heard this, I began wondering why anyone would feel like quitting. I had chosen to do this program, had no intension of quitting, knew I could make it through, and had always been a good student. They must have been talking to the other students in my cohort. My pride kicked in.

The next day we started two weeks of classes. The first class was brutal. The stress levels were high. I ended up in the emergency room the second night just checking to be sure I wasn't having a heart attack. They confirmed it was just my stomach acting up. I had never had stomach problems before. The next day I noticed those in the cohort ahead of us (we took the first two classes with the cohort ahead of us) were passing a big bottle of antacid around the room. It wasn't just me. Seeing them pass those tablets around helped calm me down.

The class ended on Saturday morning with a four-hour exam – a five-page paper proving we had learned the concepts in the class. I felt pretty good about my paper. But one student from our cohort came out and said, "I'm quitting. I just bombed that paper and I'm going back home." He lived in Texas so, if he left, he wasn't coming back. I reminded him that he had paid for both classes and he just needed to take a break over the weekend and come back the next week. He did. The second week was much less stress. This guy who wanted to quit became the fastest finisher in DBA history until someone beat him by a week the next year.

Well, the workload didn't stop and, with my duties as Dean of the School of Business, teaching, and being a husband and dad, it was brutal. It wasn't very long before I was just ready to quit the DBA program. I am not a quitter. Quitting means admitting failure and I just don't fail. Pride. But I was broken. I felt like I just couldn't do this level of academic work. I had already learned that I wasn't nearly as intelligent as most of the others in my cohort or in the cohort ahead of me and maybe I didn't deserve to be a doctor. So, I admitted this to others in my cohort. I was ready to quit. The very same guy I had encouraged to stay after the exam started encouraging me. Others did, too. It really helped. I kept going. Today, they call me doctor even though I know there are so many others who deserve the title more than I do. Pride will be broken. God uses circumstances to break us. I'm glad He did that for me.

Going through things together helps

I Thessalonians 5:11

The first time I experienced the cohort model of education was during my doctorate. The cohort model means everyone in your class starts and, hopefully, finishes together. While we didn't take every class together because there were four different doctoral tracks, we took about one-half of the classes together. The first year, we took every class together and, for four of those classes, we were in the same classroom for about five straight days and most of us stayed in the same apartment building or hotel. We got to know each other pretty well, pretty quickly.

As cohorts go, we had a pretty good one. I don't mean everyone was extremely intelligent. What I mean is we supported each other. There was a group of six of us who got especially close. We all struggled at times. Five of us had either full-time teaching jobs and one had a full-time job in industry. We were all married and all but one of us still had kids at home. Life wasn't easy.

So when one of us was struggling, we would let the others know and we would encourage each other. Sometimes it was through email, sometimes with a phone call, sometimes it was in person. But we did it because we all knew the others would encourage us when we needed the encouragement. Well, I guess it worked. All six of us finished the program.

I think this is part of what Paul was meaning in I Thessalonians 5:11. Paul was encouraging the Thessalonians to not get caught up in worldly things and fall asleep to spiritual things. But he was also telling them to encourage each other and build each other up. We all need encouragement sometimes. The problem is that sometimes no one else knows we are struggling. The cohort model helps develop strong relationships. It is the reason some academic programs, and especially difficult academic programs, often use a cohort model. More people finish if they really get to know each other. Less people finish if they feel they are on their own.

We need "cohorts" in real life, too. This could be a small group from church or a friend group. It could be people at work or a Bible study group. But we need people we can tell we are struggling when life gets tough. Social media today gives a false sense of connectedness. We have lots of "friends" but no relationships. It is pretty easy to understand why so many young people today are depressed. They have a false understanding of true friendship.

I know it can be intimidating but, if you don't already have a "cohort", start one. Just recently my wife and I did. We contacted another couple and opened the subject. Did they want to begin meeting with us every couple of weeks? They said yes and we invited a third couple to meet, too. None of us knew each other really well but we are getting there. It has been really good and we are beginning to share more openly and deeply. It is my new cohort.

Someone going before us is helpful

Hebrews 11:1 – 12:3

I was the first person from Grace College to attend the DBA program at Anderson University. It was all new to me and I was often left trying to figure out what was the best use of my time as I was completing assignments or reading the massive number of academic articles and/or books that some classes required. I was often frustrated, felt beaten up, and ready to quit (I talk about quitting in another devotional). I felt on my own.

Compare this to Mount Vernon University students. It seemed like there was at least one student from Mt. Vernon starting the program every year. There was one in my cohort, one in the cohort before mine, one in the cohort after mine, and I believe there was one two years ahead of me. They all knew each other well because they worked together at the same campus.

What I observed was they were often much more at peace than I felt. They did the work, went through the classes, graduated, and are all called doctor. They did it with so much less stress than I did it. I finally figured out why that was happening. They not only encouraged each other, they helped each other. It wasn't that they did the work for each other, they didn't. But they gave advice. The ones from earlier years knew what was going to be most important to success in a particular class and helped the ones in the later cohorts know what to read, what to study, how to prepare for exams, etc. They had gone before, experienced the life of a DBA student, and encouraged those coming behind them. It made a tremendous difference.

I believe the writer of Hebrews does a similar thing. He points out how many people have gone before and finished. He says these people who have gone before are cheering you on, setting an example, and showing you that you can finish. Just keep running the race. Keep your eyes on the end goal. Don't give up. Finish well.

Then you will be part of the group who is cheering on those who come after you.

About three years after I started my doctorate, someone else from Grace College started the DBA program at Anderson University. He wasn't doing the accounting track but he had to take many of the same courses from the same professors that I had taken. I spent time with him telling him what to concentrate on and what to not worry as much about. What to read in depth and what to skim. How to best prepare for the comprehensive exams at the end of the program. He told me a few times how much that helped him. The writer of Hebrews knew that. It helps to have encouragement from those who have gone before. I encourage you to find someone to encourage. It helps.

You have to know when to let go

Ecclesiastes 3:1

When I was asked by Grace College to get my doctorate, I talked with my wife, prayed about it, and started the program. I was Dean of the School of Business, taught 3 classes a semester, and advised about 30 students. Teaching 4 classes a semester and advising was considered a full load.

At first the load was manageable. But the Business Department began to grow and my doctoral work increased in intensity. At the same time, the number of accounting students grew which increased class sizes and increased the workload, too. I still had 5 children at home from the ages of 3 to 17 so there were athletic events, plays, concerts, and other things to attend. To boil it down, I had too much going on in my life and it was affecting my attitude, my family, and especially my wife.

I should have let something go in my work life, but I didn't. I began talking about it with my supervisor but there didn't seem to be any good solutions so I held onto everything for about two years longer than I should have. It got to the place where I wasn't sleeping well, wasn't doing well managing my family, and wasn't feeling good about my work. I just wasn't feeling good about anything. My wife finally called me on it and told me I had to give up something. The next day I wrote my resignation letter from being Dean of the School of Business. It felt good.

Ecclesiastes 3:1 says there is a time for everything. This seems to imply there is a time for doing certain things because we cannot do everything at the same time. I was trying to make time for everything, not considering that it was time to give up something. When I finally gave up something, my life improved greatly. It took a while to get back to better emotional and physical health but my life was better. I have learned that it is ok to say no to things.

There is a saying in business that if you want to get something done, find a busy person and ask them to do it. It usually works. People who keep themselves busy usually know how to manage themselves and tasks better than the average person does. But, if the person isn't careful, they can take on too much. That is what happened to me.

You have to know when to let things go. You have to know when to say no. For me, I needed to let the dean position go sooner. Are you managing your life well? Is there anything in your life that God is asking you to let go of?

The dangerous dogs don't bark

I Timothy 6:6-10

I love to bicycle. I'm talking riding 20 to 30 miles at a time and doing it pretty fast. For a few years when I was younger, I raced bicycles. It is an exhilarating experience and can be dangerous. I guess that is part of why I enjoyed it. After graduating from college, a friend asked me to bike across the United States with him and I said yes. I'm really glad I did. It was a great experience. Since then I have had a dream of biking across the U.S. with my sons. I don't believe that will happen but the four of us did bike around Michigan one summer. It was about 1,000 miles and included everything a bike tour should include: hills, rain, cold, heat, sore muscles, beautiful scenery, growing closer to those you are with.

If you bike enough, you deal with dogs. You learn there are different kinds of dogs. Some dogs will just stand there and bark. Others will run behind you and bark. Some will run at you and bark. All of these types of dogs are pretty easy to deal with. Most of them you can yell and they back off. A few you see coming and can outrun. Every once in a while, you have to stop or slow down so the dog will go away.

However, the really dangerous dogs don't bark. These are the ones you don't see or hear coming and they are beside you before you even know they are there. These dogs really scare me, not because they have surprised me, but because they are unpredictable. They haven't warned you. They want to hurt you.

There are things in life that are like dangerous dogs. Things that creep up on us and are there before we know it. We don't see them coming. Paul talks about one of these things in I Timothy 6. He says that wanting to get rich is dangerous. In our culture, we usually don't see this coming. We are just living a pretty normal life, we think, taking the next promotion or job change, living out the American Dream, and, one day, it hits us that we have been caught up in wanting to get rich. We didn't see it coming and it is dangerous. Paul says it causes us to fall into temptation, it traps us, and it can plunge us into ruin and destruction. That is pretty serious stuff.

So, what can we do about this? Just as in biking, we need to constantly be on the lookout. If we don't constantly keep looking for dogs when we are biking, we are sure to not see them coming unless they bark. If we aren't constantly looking for the signs of wanting to get rich, we won't see it coming. If we often think about the next nicer car, house, vacation, etc., it is a pretty clear sign we are falling into the trappings of getting rich. The problem is, this dangerous dog doesn't usually bark! It sneaks up on us quietly.

Loosening up

Ephesians 6:4

My son and I were on our bicycle trip around Indiana. I was riding the 30 year-old bike I had used to bicycle across the United States when I was 22. It was a solid bike. In preparation for the trip, I took it to a bike shop and had the wheels trued and some parts replaced to make it more suitable to my age. Even though I had biked through the southern Rocky Mountains on this bike when I was 22, at 54 years old, I knew I wouldn't be able to use the same gearing and make it around the state. Southern Indiana has some "hills" but they can be pretty steep at times; not long but steep. I'm really glad I had my bike upgraded.

My son had a newer bike that he had only owned for a couple of years. It was much lighter than mine and had better gearing. It was ready to go – so we thought. We were about 300 miles into the trip and I was biking behind my son. I noticed his rear wheel was wobbling a little so we stopped, got out the spoke wrench, and began to adjust the spokes. We fixed the wobble and started biking again.

It wasn't too far before there was a loud pop and one of his spokes had broken on his rear wheel. Right then I knew what had happened and it was my fault. You see, when I was adjusting the spokes, the only thing I did was tighten up spokes to pull the wheel into true: bad idea. The better way would have been to loosen spokes a little. By tightening, I had put too much pressure on the tighter spokes and one of them broke. It was on the cog (gearing) side of the rear wheel and we couldn't fix it ourselves. So, I loosened some spokes and we made it to a bike shop.

As Paul says in Ephesians 6, fathers are not to exasperate their children. I have seven children and sometimes tell people that God gave me so many children so I had more chances to be a better father. I still don't get it right sometimes but I'm getting a little better at loosening up rather than tightening down. Today, I believe I was way too tight with my boys. Sometimes I just expected too much out of my boys. I was tightening down instead of loosening up. This takes skill. I'm not suggesting we go against biblical principles in raising our children. Sometimes there needs to be some tension in the relationship. Think of a bike wheel. If all the spokes are really loose, you can't bike anywhere. The wheel won't go around. But if the spokes are all too tight, they eventually break. It is this way with children. If we are too tight with them, they eventually break. Finding the balance between discipline and freedom is tricky but it is what Paul is talking about.

Where to focus

James 4:13-17

I was in the middle of a 10-day bicycle trip around Indiana with my third son. It was the summer after he graduated from college and we had limited time to make the 600 miles we had planned for the trip. We were taking a counterclockwise circle around the state and happened to be in the southwest corner heading toward Bedford, Indiana. I had traveled all around Indiana for a job I had earlier in my work career but had never been in this part of the state. It was rural, rural, rural! Hills, farms, woods, windy roads. It felt like Nowhere, Indiana.

We had stopped at a gas station to eat lunch and met an older couple on a motorcycle. They suggested we take a scenic route that would probably cut some time off our trip and would have less traffic. It sounded appealing so we went for it. It was just like they described it. Beautiful country, windy road, no traffic, several very small towns. Sort of a perfect road for bike touring.

We were 20 or so miles into this ride and I heard a thud. My son had hit something and broke a spoke. We didn't have the tools with us to fix it. It was Saturday afternoon and we were at least 20 miles from Bedford. So, he pulled out his smart phone to check for the nearest bike shop. Remember, we are in Nowhere, Indiana which means no cell service. No traffic. No people. The perfect storm.

I was frustrated. My son was frustrated. So, I asked how he was so stupid to hit something like that (I probably didn't say "stupid" but I know I thought it). It was then he admitted that he wasn't paying attention to what was just in front of him but he was looking around and too far ahead. He didn't see the trouble right in front of him and hit it. We "limped" his bike into Bedford. Thankfully, my son happened to have a friend living in the area who took us to a bike shop in Bloomington which opened up just to fix his spoke. Everything ended well but could have been avoided.

This reminds me of how I live life sometimes. We get so fixated on the future and things we want to happen or achieve that we lose focus on the present and mess up. God wants us to live in the present. We need to have an understanding of the future so we know where we are headed, but if we focus on the future too much, we mess up the present. Many parents can't wait until the empty nest part of life or retirement that they don't enjoy the present. Then, when the future is realized, they regret how they didn't really live their lives well.

It isn't always living for the future that messes up the present. Sometimes it is "living" in the past. I've been there. Overall, I had a good past with many things about it I liked. But, if I wish I were back there and fixate on that time of my life, I miss living well in the present. There is no way to get the present back. Live it well now!

Thirsty

John 6:35 & Revelations 21:5

The summer after my senior year of college, I took a coast-to-coast bicycle trip from San Diego, California to Tybee Island, Georgia. It was a great 3,000 mile bike trip. I learned a lot about this great country in the six weeks it took us to make the trip. One thing I learned is how vast and desolate the western United States can be. When we planned the trip, we decided to not set any specific agenda but just bike east. So, we decided to visit Grand Canyon. If you haven't been there, I recommend it. It is massive! I had seen pictures and movies but nothing compares to seeing it live. After we froze for one night there (the south rim is still over 7,000 feet high), we coasted for close to 30 or 40 miles as we went down into the painted desert.

The painted desert ended and it was just desert; a lot of nothing and really hot. Since it is illegal to bike along an interstate highway, we needed to bike on other roads through the desert. The route for the day was over 100 miles long and there was just one town along the way. We would need to make sure we filled up with water at the town so we could make it through the desert.

We started out early in the morning and the biking was good; few cars and lots of open space. We didn't see much at all. We passed a house or two, then a couple of houses with a small building, and then nothing. After about 10 miles or so of the nothing, we realized the couple of houses with the small building had been the town. We had missed it! We discussed turning around and biking back but we knew that would probably mean we couldn't get to the next town before dark. We needed to go on and we didn't have much water left.

The next several hours were interesting. I had seen movies where someone was out in the desert without water and started seeing things. It began happening to me. I would look out over the desert and could see a lake. I knew there wasn't a lake there but I saw a lake. After a while, the only thing I could think about was water. This was before the days of cell phones and GPS so we didn't really know how far we had to bike before we hit the next town. I was fixated on water. Any time I tried to think about something else, my mind came back to water. It consumed me. Well, we made it to the next town and stopped at the first place we came to, a restaurant I believe, and got water. Of course, we drank and drank.

Jesus talked about drinking and never being thirsty again. Are you thirsty? I think God wants us to be thirsty for Him just as I was so thirsty in the desert. Am I consumed with thirst for Him? Do my thoughts continually come back to Him? We still have to keep biking through life but are we consumed with our desire for God? Often, I'm not. I get distracted and caught up in the things of life that really aren't that important. I need to be more consumed with drinking from His well.

Compassion

Mark 3:1-5

My son and I were into the last couple of days of our bike trip and had stopped for the night at Whitewater Memorial State Park near Liberty, Indiana for the night. It was a special night because my son's fiancé was bringing us supper. The meal was fantastic. Much better than the stuff I would have cooked up for us that night.

We knew a big storm was coming in the next morning and we were a little scared. On a bicycle, you don't have many options in the rain. You either just sit somewhere and wait it out which messes up your schedule or you bike in the rain. If it is a light rain and decently warm, biking in the rain works.

We had just packed up our tent and loaded our bikes when the rain hit us the next morning. We quickly biked to a shelter at the park and waited. But it began looking like it was going to rain for a long time. So, we decided to bike to the entrance of the park and ask for some help. The entry gate was first so we stopped there. I got off my bike, entered the small enclosure to get out of the rain, and asked the aged man working if he would check the weather radar for us to see where the storm was at and how long we would have to wait before the rain stopped.

Shockingly, he kicked me out of the building and back into the rain! He knew we were on bikes but wouldn't let us stay in the building. We had to stand out of the rain! He said something about those were the rules. Then, he told us he wouldn't help us. I was mad. I was already wet, a little cold, and here was a state employee refusing to help; my taxes pay his salary! Talk about no compassion! So, we decided to bike back into the park and wait. At that point, he told us that if we tried to reenter the park, he would charge us another entry fee! Those were the rules. If I could have, I would have fired him on the spot. We decided to bike to the ranger center and ask for help. The lady at the desk was happy to help us. It ended up being a rainy day and we didn't make as many miles as we wanted.

Rules versus compassion. Jesus seemed to know when compassion was more important than rules. Mark 3 demonstrates his attitude when he healed a man on the Sabbath. Rules are important. They help keep order and maintain an orderly society. But sometimes, rules need to be broken and compassion is more important.

Some final devotionals

These devotionals are ones I rarely have time to use during a class. They are topics I often discuss with students during classes but not during a devotional time.

No work, no food

II Thessalonians 3:6-10

My wife and I have seven living children. One thing we consistently tried to apply to each child was our rule on work. If you didn't work, you didn't eat. Before you shut me down and think I was a horrible parent, lack of work meant missing one meal. Each of our children have missed one meal and a couple of them have missed another meal on a different occasion. Some children just learned faster than others that Mom and Dad were serious that everyone helps when we have work to do. I found it interesting that the older children would begin encouraging the younger ones to actually work. There was both a level of compassion not wanting their sibling to miss a meal as well as wanting the sibling to actually help.

As parents, we knew that missing one meal would not damage our children in any way. Also, we personally choose to fast at times and know how it feels to be hungry. It isn't comfortable. We wanted our children to find out how that felt if they chose to not help with picking up sticks in the yard, raking leaves, or some of the other tasks we did together as a family.

Our family rule has a biblical backing. In II Thessalonians 3, Paul tells the Thessalonians that if someone was not willing to work, then they should not eat. In other words, don't give handouts to people who are lazy.

In Paul's day, the government did not help poor people. If someone was poor, their relatives helped. Once Christians began meeting as churches, the church would also help. This is why Paul gave guidelines about who should be helped and who should not be helped. One thing was clear, helping people who were lazy was not really helping them. It was hurting them. If they had the ability to work and still asked for handouts, they should not be helped until they were willing to work.

One principle my wife and I have tried to continually keep in mind is that we are/were raising adults, not children. We had children in our house but we were doing things to help them become productive adults not keep them in the mindset of children. Teaching college as I now do, I come across some students who still have a child's mindset. These students think I should do many things for them. I fear their parents had a mindset that they were raising children. When taken in the context of raising adults, our rule of working to eat seems to fit and I'm glad we stuck to it even when our children complained.

Value of the church

And let us consider how we may spur one another on toward love and good deeds, not giving up meeting together, as some are in the habit of doing, but encouraging one another—and all the more as you see the Day approaching. Hebrews 10:24, 25

In this passage, the writer of Hebrews gives a reason for why the church is valuable for Christians. Often, I hear people quote or refer to verse 25 only. The first part of verse 25 is an encouragement to keep meeting together. I think most of us give a specific interpretation as this verse meaning we should go to church. While I don't disagree that going to church is a good practice, I believe there is more to these two verses than just attending church. In the United States, we see many people attending church but not really doing what Hebrews 10:24, 25 states.

I believe verse 25 must be taken in the context of verse 24. Hebrews 10:24 states, "And let us consider how we may spur one another on toward love and good deeds…" Hebrews 10:25 then states, "…not giving up meeting together, as some are in the habit of doing, but encouraging one another – and all the more as you see the Day approaching." The context of going to church is so we may encourage each other to not give up love and good deeds. Just going to church to say we have met the requirement of "not giving up meeting together" does not accomplish what the writer of Hebrews envisioned.

During my life, I will admit that I have been involved in both types of churches – ones which become interested and involved in my life and one which was mostly a Sunday morning meeting. The "Sunday only" church had great teaching. Our pastor was one of the best I have ever heard at taking a passage of scripture, explaining it in context, and making it relevant to today. I still value things I learned and understand better because of those sermons, but that is where it ended. We did not meet with anyone other than on Sunday mornings. We did not talk with others very often or get involved in their lives. We never really learned to know people at a level where we could trust them with our lives, speak into their lives, or allow them to speak into our lives. It was belonging to a church without really becoming the church and something was missing.

Two other churches we have been part of have been different. One was during the time when our fifth child was in the hospital and, eventually, died. That church was so very involved in our lives. They prayed for and with us. They watched our children. They provided meals for us. One 16-year old girl who was being homeschooled even lived with us so she could help with our children and care for our home when we were caring for our sick daughter. That girl is now a missionary and we support her family financially. Her caring actions deeply impacted our lives. She really was the church to us and encouraged us to love and good deeds.

Another church is the one we now attend. We had recently started attending the church when my wife had a cancer scare. I was amazed how quickly women from that church surrounded my wife with love and care. The amount of love and good deeds that seemed to happen quickly and naturally was impressive. It helped to solidify our belief that this was a healthy church. Several years have passed and we are still impressed with the amount of caring and encouraging that is present. People within our church have struggles but we gather around each other and support each other.

In a generation where social media fights to take people away from meeting together, face-to-face church is still important. I know the writer of Hebrews didn't have a clue there would be an internet but he/she knew that Christians meeting together and encouraging each other to love and good deeds was a timeless message.

Things my dad did not teach me

Proverbs 22:6

My dad died rather suddenly in 2006 when he was 73. It wasn't that we expected him to live until age 73. He had a heart attack when he was 50, had triple bypass surgery that same year, and an on-demand pacemaker installed the next year. Since both my great-grandfather and my grandfather on my dad's side of the family had died from heart attacks when they were also about 50 years old, my dad having heart issues was not unexpected. At age 73, my dad was experiencing some fatigue and knew it was his heart. During the procedure to install a stent, a blood vessel in his brain burst and he died. We hadn't expected his death to be in this manner so it was a little of a shock.

When preparing for his Celebration of Life (memorial service) and me being an educator, I decided to say some things related to how my dad taught me and decided to title it, "Things my dad did not teach me." The following are the five things I said:

1. Be lazy. My dad made us work. We always lived in the country when I was growing up and we usually had animals. When I was really young, we farmed and that meant being part of feeding animals and "helping" around the farm. Later, it was shoveling manure, cutting weeds out of the beans, fixing fence – you get the picture. We worked pretty hard compared to many of my school friends. But my dad had a balance. We also were allowed to play sports during school, be part of our youth group, etc. It was a good balance. I learned to work hard and play hard.
2. Swear. I never heard my dad swear. I never heard my dad use words that were considered inappropriate for a Christian person to use. It deeply affected me and was something I always appreciated about my dad. He wasn't a perfect

person and I have turned out not to be a perfect person. But he set a great example on what it meant to hold your tongue.

3. Buy more than I need. There were times during my life when I thought my dad needed to get rid of some of the older stuff he was still using and buy something newer. One of the things he and I enjoyed doing together was to fish. My dad had a very old fishing pole. I thought he needed a newer pole. But when I suggested him buying a newer one, he said, "What for? Why would I need that?" My dad knew the secret of being content with what was good enough.

4. Just read my Bible on Sunday. My dad taught me that the Bible was a book for every day, not just Sunday. Our family read the Bible every day at breakfast. It was something that irked me sometimes when I was young and something I deeply appreciate now. Not only did my dad read the Bible to us at breakfast, he knew the Bible really well. Any time we had any kind of Bible question come up, he seemed to know the answer. That has challenged me throughout my life.

5. Compromise on my beliefs. My dad would "fight" for what he believed was right. He wasn't a wordy person and could sit through meetings without feeling the need to speak. But when he finally did speak, people listened. I learned from that. If you want to be taken seriously, it is better to speak less frequently and make sure you have something to contribute when you speak. When I was still a child, I experienced my dad walking away from a very profitable business he owned to make sure he did not compromise on what he believed. His partner was not being totally honest in some dealings and my dad walked away rather than be part of dishonesty. It continues to impact me.

These were the five things I shared as we remembered my dad's life. I want to be known by my children for both good things I do and for the not so good things I do not do.

31092521R00060

Made in the USA
Middletown, DE
28 December 2018